© Hudson's Bay Company
© 2011 Assouline Publishing
601 West 26th Street, 18th floor
New York, NY 10001, USA
Tel.: 212 989-6810   Fax: 212 647-0005
www.assouline.com

ISBN: 9782 75940 5015

Printed in China

SINCE

DEPUIS

1670

ASSOULINE

FOREWORD

For me, indeed for many Canadians, the mere sight of a Hudson's Bay Point Blanket brings back a flood of childhood memories: of hockey, Mounties, Stephen Leacock, frozen feet, runny noses, and, if you are of a certain age, *The Plouffe Family*, Friday nights at 8:30. Even if you have no idea who Gump Worsley, Bernie Faloney, or even Wayne and Shuster were, chances are you've probably seen one of the blankets. They are generally off-white and have four coloured stripes: green, red, yellow, and indigo. In one corner of the blanket are the "points": black half-foot-long lines, varying from one to eight in number. They were a buyer's shorthand for the blanket's size, with one being the smallest and eight being the largest. Originally used in trade with the natives for pelts, they were as thick as plywood and pretty much waterproof.

For those fortunate enough to have had a Canadian childhood in the balmy decades after the war, the Hudson's Bay stores and outposts were as symbolic of a city's arrival as sports arenas are now. The stores themselves were massive Edwardian temples in the cities along the nation's railroad lines, such as Winnipeg,

Saskatoon, Edmonton, Calgary, Vancouver, and Victoria, and back in the day, they sold everything under their own name, from hard liquor to canvas-covered canoes. When I was in my teens, the company shortened the logos on the stores to the then more modern-looking The Bay—or La Baie, for people in Quebec. This did not sit well with old-timers, who loved the rugged, storied, 300-year history of the Hudson's Bay Company.

We had dozens of the blankets in our house when I was growing up. They were the last vestiges of my grandfather's trading post. Like the men who founded the Hudson's Bay Company, he was an Englishman who followed the call of the wild and sailed across the Atlantic in search of adventure and fortune. The latter eluded him, but from his trading post in Moose Jaw, Saskatchewan, he sold pelts to the big company, and years later off-loaded the whole caboodle and moved east. Miles from my grandfather's life, and years and years away from his days as a trapper, my wife and I sleep under a Point Blanket on winter nights in Greenwich Village. For me, it is a link to my past; it is my madeleine.

GRAYDON CARTER

Hudson's Bay Company York Boats at Norway House by Walter J. Phillips

THE COMPANY THAT BECAME A NATION

For nearly three and a half centuries its presence has loomed large over the northern half of North America. From its earliest days, in a few small outposts on the barren, windy shores of a huge inland sea, until the present, with retail operations spanning the continent from coast to coast, the hemisphere's oldest business carries on. It is a piece of living history, a link to a storied past. It is the Company of Adventurers Trading into Hudson's Bay, the Hudson's Bay Company: the company that became a nation.

There is nothing else quite like Hudson's Bay Company anywhere. It helped to define the geography of Canada and carry British culture to its farthest corners. The Company's history is inextricably woven with that of the country. Its people are Canada's historic figures; its places are our cities and towns; its colours are our colours. It is part of Canada, and we are part of it.

How did this happen? How did a trading company become the custodian of half a continent? How did its business evolve from fur pelts to high fashion? How did a British concern become so thoroughly Canadian? And how does the special relationship between the Company and the country continue, to this day, to inspire both?

It is hard to imagine that the original adventurers and investors who founded Hudson's Bay Company had any real idea of what they were getting themselves into. At best they saw an interesting business opportunity and seized it. A cadre of wealthy and influential Londoners, active in both politics and finance, backed a speculative voyage to North America promoted by a pair of charismatic Frenchmen. Pierre-Esprit Radisson and his brother-in-law Médard Chouart, Sieur de Groseilliers, proposed a radical idea: to bypass New France and trade into the heart of the continent by establishing a new route via Hudson Bay. The British were their last chance. Attempts to secure backing from the French and the New Englanders had failed.

The timing was inauspicious. Plague had broken out in London and the City was dealing with the aftermath of the Great Fire of 1666. The Court had retired to the country to avoid both.

The intrepid Frenchmen followed. There they were introduced to a few key players, including the King's favourite cousin, Prince Rupert of the Rhine. A Renaissance man, Rupert was a professional soldier, an artist, a part-time scientist and inventor, and a canny businessman with a growing portfolio. He liked what he heard.

Well, why not? Fur was a lucrative business, a key commodity that yielded felt for the important hat industry. Europe needed a new supply of beaver, having extinguished its own, and North America seemed to be infested with the animals. Cold, northerly origins would mean thicker, better quality fur. Moreover Hudson Bay, discovered more than half a century before but still little-explored, led straight to the supply. Soon a small group had put up some money, acquired a pair of ships, and purchased an inventory of goods to trade.

The ships set sail down the Thames in June of 1668. Weeks later one was damaged in a storm off the coast of Ireland and turned back home "with some losse." The second, the *Nonsuch*, carried on alone. It made landfall at the mouth of a large river its crew named for their royal patron, Prince Rupert. The small outpost they built to shelter themselves for the winter they named Charles Fort, after their sovereign, King Charles II.

In the spring of 1669 the Cree who lived round about came down to the Bay to trade with the newcomers. The exchange was successful, and by summer the *Nonsuch* had embarked on the homeward journey, her holds brimming with the finest quality furs. In October she was spotted sailing up the Thames, her return met with delight by the investors, who soon covered their costs and made a small profit. The business model proven, it was time to formalize their venture.

With the active participation of Prince Rupert, the King was asked to provide a charter to the new company. Charters, granted by the Crown for specific commercial ends, were all the rage. They gave such endeavours prominence and credibility—things that shareholders in the newfangled joint stock companies looked for. Moreover a charter allowed the Crown to promote its own expansionist policies at someone else's expense.

And so it was that on May 2, 1670, King Charles II granted a Royal Charter and trading monopoly over the entire Hudson Bay drainage basin to the "Governor and Company of Adventurers of England trading into Hudson's Bay." The King named his "dear and entirely beloved cousin Prince Rupert" as the Company's first Governor, overseeing the territory henceforth to be known as "Rupert's Land." An area comprising over 1.5 million square miles, from Labrador in the east to the Rockies in the west, north to the Arctic and south to modern-day Minnesota and North Dakota, it comprised more than forty percent of modern Canada. Although no one could have known it at the time, it was the largest land transaction in the history of the world. And the Charter gave the Company much more than just a trading monopoly. Its clauses outlined the rights and obligations of the Company of Adventurers over their new domain, such as the right to exploit mineral resources and the obligation to search for the Northwest Passage.

The vastness of Rupert's Land and the potential of the Charter's terms were beyond imagining—no one had any real idea of either. In fact it would be more than a century before the Company got around to opening its first post inland, away from Hudson Bay's shores. Until then, "asleep by the frozen sea," HBC settled into the comfortable rhythms of the annual trade cycle.

Despite how routine that business became, the impact of the fur trade was enormous. It brought together two distinct cultures in a relationship based on mutual benefit. The Cree taught the first European traders essential skills for surviving in the harsh environment. They also caught the beaver and fox that sustained the trade, trapping the animals, skinning them, and delivering pelts, the highly valuable raw material required to sustain a thriving manufacturing business. In exchange the First Nations received key manufactured goods: metal kettles, needles, and knives; firearms, powder, and shot; blankets and cloth, buttons and beads. Each culture had something of value to the other, something the other needed and wanted. It was this fact that made the trade so important and ensured its longevity.

Other kinds of exchange also occurred. Europeans adopted First Nations technology such as canoes, snowshoes, moccasins, and toboggans, as well as foodstuffs like wild rice and pemmican, the mixture of dried meat, fat, and berries that became the staple diet of the inland fur trade in the west. Social interactions between the two groups led to the creation of the Métis, sometimes called the "children of the fur trade." The resulting multicultural community attained the highest social status, as exemplified by British Columbia's first Governor (of Scottish and Barbadian heritage) and his wife (of Irish, French Canadian, and Cree heritage), Sir James and Lady Amelia Douglas. They prefigure the multiracial, multiethnic Canada of today.

It has been said that the letters HBC stand for "Here Before Canada," which says something about the Company and its relationship to the land. Hudson's Bay Company has been here since before Canada was Canada—before it developed into the Canada we know today. The Company provided some of the country's most intrepid explorers, men such as Henry Kelsey, Anthony Henday, Samuel Hearne, John Rae, and the great cartographer David Thompson, who learned his craft while working for HBC. These men travelled extensively, contributing to the growing body of scientific knowledge about the immensity of the country, its geography, peoples, animals, and plants.

HBC also shaped the country in other, subtler ways. The Company often set up shop in traditional gathering places. This ensured good trade. As native populations took jobs with the Company as hunters, guides, interpreters, and seamstresses, their camps became more and more permanent. Towns such as Fort Langley and Edmonton arose spontaneously around their posts. In the far north, where the Inuit were nomadic well into the twentieth century, the effect of the Company on the pattern of settlement is even more evident. Iqaluit, Baker Lake, and Gjoa Haven are among the communities established by Hudson's Bay Company.

One of the terms of the Charter was to encourage settlement. This was a political—rather than economic—goal. For many years the Company simply ignored it, and with good reason. The fur trade and colonization were not symbiotic. The first thing settlers did was clear the land for agriculture, thereby eliminating the habitats of most fur-bearing animals. Large numbers of people also tended to overhunt, further stressing animal populations. But some trends are irresistible.

In the late 1700s, a group of Montreal businessmen calling themselves the North West Company challenged HBC's monopoly by heading into the frontier, blazing new trails throughout the northwest. After a period of fierce competition, the two rivals merged in 1821, leaving the Company larger, stronger, and more dynamic, with control of an even vaster network of trading posts and forts stretching from the far north to the plains and the Pacific coast.

Meanwhile, population density was increasing at centres like the Red River Settlement. Founded in 1811 by shareholder Lord Selkirk on land purchased from the Company, it became the nucleus for the first of Canada's western provinces. Beyond the mountains, HBC leased all of Vancouver Island from the Crown, in return for encouraging settlement and administering the resulting colony.

By the latter half of the 1800s, the fur trade was in decline. Fur hats, replaced by silk, were going out of fashion. Meanwhile, in eastern Canada—long settled by both the French and the English—responsible government had taken hold. Britain's remaining

North American colonies longed for independence, which the Crown, tired of their expense and distraction, was eager to promote. As the inexorable march towards Confederation unfolded, the parties agreed on one thing: Rupert's Land and the North West Territory could not remain a private fiefdom administered by Hudson's Bay Company. They needed to be available to the new country for its western expansion. Six months after Canada's creation, William McDougall, a Father of Confederation, declared in the House of Commons: "If we don't expand, we must contract."

After a period of negotiation, the Company signed the Deed of Surrender, which took effect in 1870 and instantly transformed the very nature of its operations. HBC returned the stewardship of its traditional territories to the Crown, which turned them over to the new Canadian state. In return the Company received a settlement of £300,000 cash; land grants of one-twentieth of all the land in the "Fertile Belt" (stretching from Lake of the Woods in modern-day northwestern Ontario, to the Rocky Mountains in Alberta); and an additional 50,000 acres of land surrounding its trading posts. While the final cash price was much less than the Company wanted, the lands it received proved far more valuable.

As immigrants poured into Canada, it was land they craved. A new business, selling real estate to settlers who followed the new railroads across the west, would provide the lion's share of Company profits for the next fifty years.

With the end of the fur trade and the opening of the west came the beginning of the retail era. Business was now conducted for cash, not for pelts. And Hudson's Bay Company did not lack customers. Settlers, prospectors seeking their fortune in the gold fields of British Columbia and the Yukon, and those living in the growing towns and cities all needed goods, which the Company was only too happy to supply.

The twentieth century saw Hudson's Bay Company expand across the country. In the west, its traditional home, trading posts developed into Company stores. As urbanization increased demand for luxury items and new fashions, it built a series of large metropolitan department stores in Calgary, Edmonton,

Victoria, Vancouver, Saskatoon, and Winnipeg between the years 1913 and 1926. These multi-storey retail palaces became social hubs of their cities, centres of commerce, and much more, offering fine dining, concerts, exhibitions, and lectures.

These western urban flagships positioned the Company for the postwar prosperity of the 1950s and beyond. Elsewhere it grew through strategic acquisition of established businesses. Premium retailers like Morgan's of Montreal (est. 1845) and Simpsons of Toronto (est. 1872) were brought into the HBC fold, and helped to cement its reputation in central and eastern markets.

Meanwhile, the Company's operations became increasingly directed from Canada. By the time British tax law necessitated a change to the location of its headquarters, its Canadianization was almost complete. In 1970, after three centuries as a Canadian icon, Hudson's Bay Company officially became a Canadian corporation. Within four years the profile of its shareholders had shifted overwhelmingly from British to Canadian.

The legacy of Hudson's Bay Company cannot be underestimated. Thanks to HBC, British Columbia is part of Canada. The Arctic coastline and much of the west were mapped by HBC men who risked life and limb to explore them. HBC ships opened the waters of the Arctic archipelago and the Mackenzie River. For more than half of the twentieth century, anyone venturing north of sixty degrees—be it the RCMP, the Geological Survey, or the military—had to call on the Company for support or assistance. For a very long time HBC delivered not only the mail, but the constable, the priest, and the nurse as well.

Across the prairies, people bought their farmsteads from Hudson's Bay Company. In the towns that grew up around the former posts, newcomers purchased lots on which they would build their homes. In some places, like Edmonton, people could buy both the lot and a house, designed and built by the Company. Many Canadians still live, till the soil, and raise families on land originally purchased from HBC.

Over the years, Hudson's Bay Company has employed thousands, and provided goods and services to thousands more. Today it employs 50,000 people at more than 600 retail outlets. Its businesses include the flagship chain The Bay, as well as Zellers, Home Outfitters, and Fields. Its products and brands have become household names—none more than the famous HBC Point Blanket, a product with origins in the fur trade and a pedigree hundreds of years old. Generations of Canadians have slept under its familiar stripes and worn outerwear made from its wool cloth. Known the world over, it is synonymous with Hudson's Bay Company and with Canada.

Modern companies spend thousands of dollars each year developing and promoting their brands or, even more daunting, creating brands from scratch. With its long history and special relationship to Canada, HBC is in a unique position of having a brand—of being a brand—that Canadians recognize and respond to almost viscerally. Today Hudson's Bay Company signifies many things, among them quality, reliability, fashion, and value. But above that, it represents an unparalleled heritage, a cultural legacy, and a living history, which it shares with all Canadians.

The company that became a nation, indeed.

A
ADVENTURE

Born in an era of exploration, Hudson's Bay Company's early history is a litany of epic journeys and intrepid individuals which together have made a lasting mark on Canada. Today that legacy of adventure continues to express itself in new and exciting ways. Engaging special events, exhibits and personal appearances create unique customer experiences that elevate shopping out of the ordinary and into the realm of the special.

N
NONSUCH

The ship that launched the Hudson's Bay Company, the *Nonsuch* sailed to Hudson Bay in 1668 and returned to London the following year bearing a rich cargo of furs from the New World. It's not known what became of this famous ketch, but since she was too small to be used as a full-time trading vessel, she was likely sold.

J

JOURNAL

In flowing, handwritten script, the story of Hudson's Bay Company unfolds in the journals of the Company factors who ran its outposts. Today these meticulous diaries are considered invaluable heritage artifacts that chart the growth of the Company and of Canada.

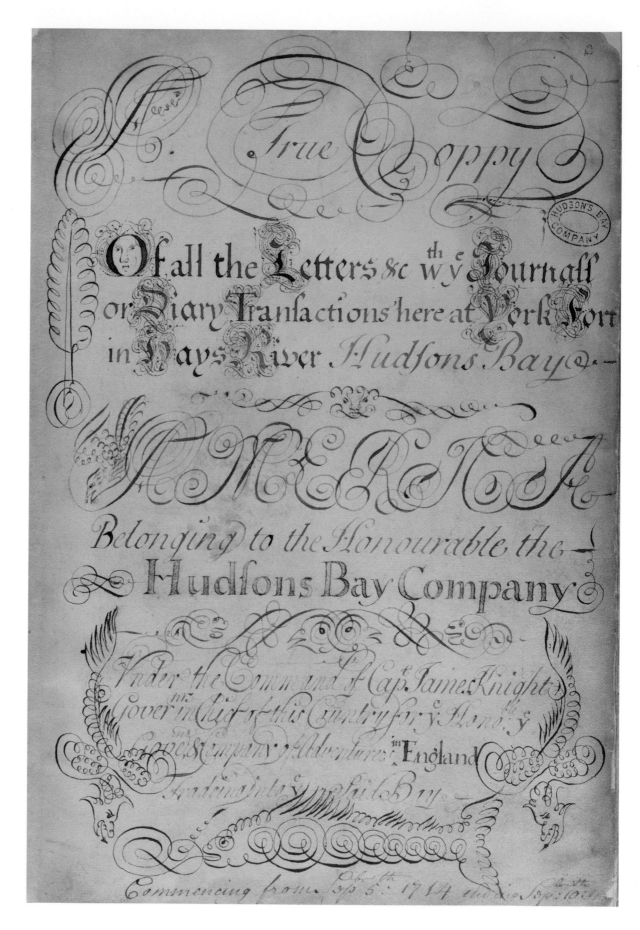

R
PRINCE RUPERT

A Renaissance man of the Restoration, Prince Rupert of the Rhine knew a good deal when he saw one. His persuasive personality helped convince his cousin King Charles II to grant Hudson's Bay Company its Royal Charter, and appoint Rupert as its first Governor.

B

THE BAY

The Bay is the Hudson's Bay Company's full line department store banner. With over 90 locations from coast to coast, Bay stores focus on high fashion merchandise in apparel, accessories and home décor at mid to upper price points. Located in suburban and urban markets, The Bay enjoys a dominant position in the downtown cores of Canada's major cities, such as Queen St. in Toronto (this page) and Calgary (opposite).

Hudson's Bay Company

R

RIVERS

Hudson's Bay Company Chief Trader Archibald McDonald holds on as his men paddle the Fraser River rapids in 1828 (opposite). Laced by networks of rivers and lakes, Canada's natural landscape made travel by paddle and canoe the most practical way into the country's interior.

Postal Card

SPACE FOR CORRESPONDENCE   ADDRESS SPACE ONE

MADE IN "Royalty Series" CANADA
CANADIAN ROYALTIES LIMITED TORONTO

Dear Mom & Dad
Heres the store
that we spent shours
in and didn't we half
of it something nice
for you. It is nice
up here today. It
was raining cats &
dogs last night.
Love
Merryha

Mrs. & Mr. J. Mandell
1288 Lupton Ave.
San Jose.
Calif.

(116) HUDSON'S BAY CO. DEPT. STORE VANCOUVER, B.C., CANADA.

P
POSTCARD

Shopping at a flagship department store was the highlight of many a trip to the city in the early days of retail. No visit was complete without picking up a company postcard and mailing it to friends and family back home. Since most department stores also featured postal outlets, the cards could be bought, signed and sent on the spot.

R
RELIABILITY

Driver Roy McLean hands her parcel to Mrs. Rive less than 24 hours after she ordered it. Meeting—or exceeding—customer expectations for efficient service are no less important today than they were in 1961, when this photograph was taken.

F

FASHION SHOW

At the elegant Arcadian Court, Toronto's high society gathers in 1929 to view the season's newest styles. In-house fashion shows have always been an important part of Hudson's Bay Company's allure, offering the public an early opportunity to catch the latest trends before they hit the streets.

D

DISCOVERY

Built in 1901, the HMS *Discovery* sailed into the history books during Captain Robert Falcon Scott's famous Antarctic voyage of 1901–1904. Purchased by the Hudson's Bay Company in 1905, the ship carried goods and supplies for the fur trade for almost two decades—one of many legendary Hudson's Bay Company vessels that helped link communities throughout the North.

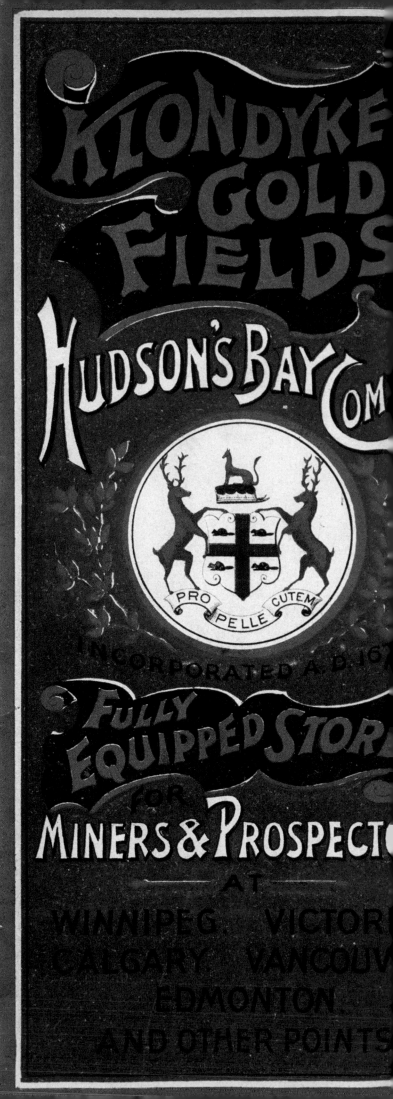

G

GOLD RUSH

They came by the thousands, hoping to strike the mother lode. In 1898 men from every corner of the world flocked to the Yukon to stake their claims in the Klondike gold fields. For Hudson's Bay Company they were a brand new pool of customers who needed everything from clothing to tools to foodstuffs—all of which the Company was happy to provide.

L
LUXE

The Bay relaunched The Room, its designer fashion department, in October 2009. The stunning design, by noted firm Yabu Pushelberg, won the 2009 Retail Design Institute (RDI) International Store Design Award for Store of the Year.

H
HOLLYWOOD

Lights, cameras . . . action! In 1941, Hudson's Bay
Company got the Hollywood treatment thanks to
a lavish Twentieth Century-Fox film titled *Hudson's
Bay*. Starring Paul Muni, Laird Cregar, Vincent Price,
and Gene Tierney, it tells the story of the Company's
founding in 1670.

E
EXHIBIT

As an integral part of community life, department stores often hosted major events, such as fashion shows, concerts, art displays, and trade shows. Shortly before it opened, in 1929, the Arcadian Court in Toronto hosted the city's first car show.

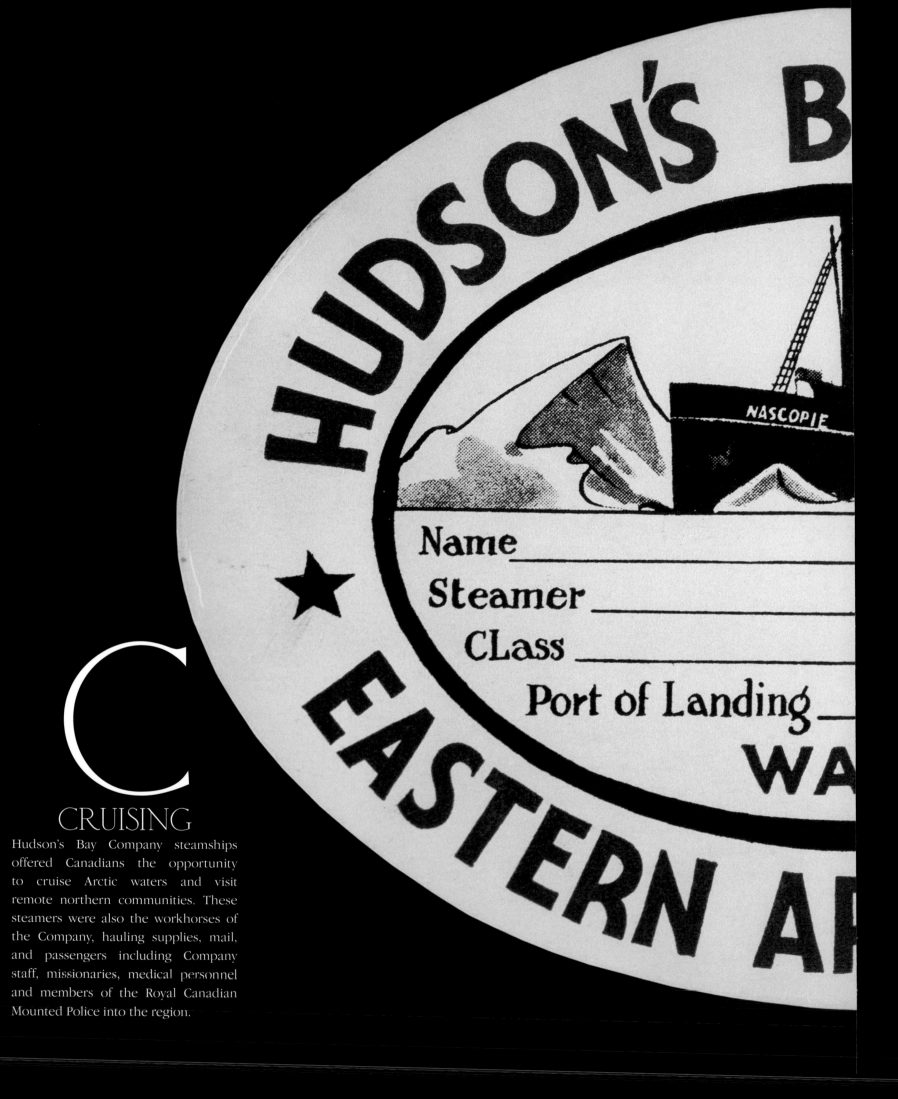

HUDSON'S B

EASTERN AR

NASCOPIE

Name _____
Steamer _____
CLass _____

Port of Landing _____

WA

CRUISING

Hudson's Bay Company steamships offered Canadians the opportunity to cruise Arctic waters and visit remote northern communities. These steamers were also the workhorses of the Company, hauling supplies, mail, and passengers including Company staff, missionaries, medical personnel and members of the Royal Canadian Mounted Police into the region.

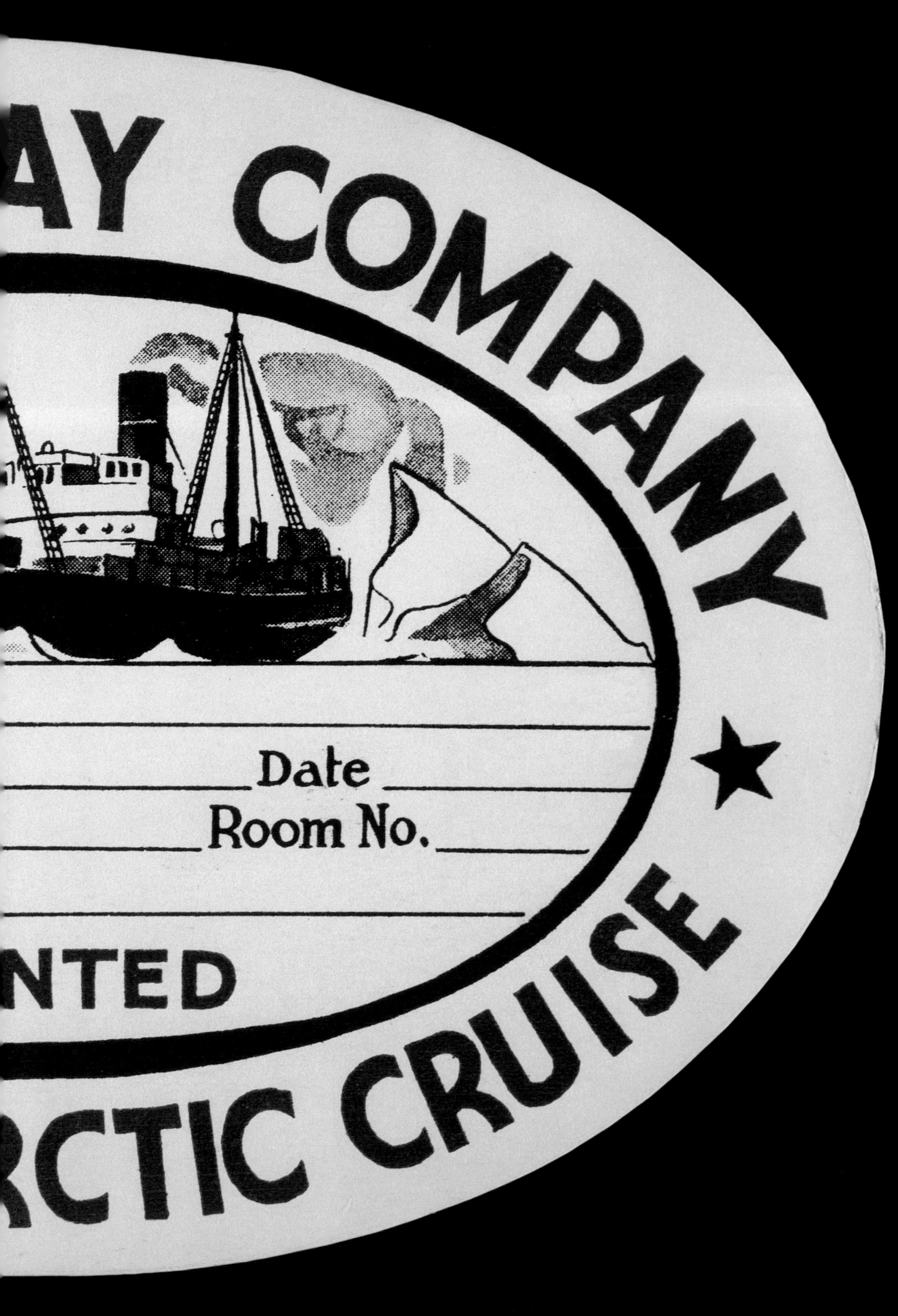
AY COMPANY
Date
Room No.
NTED
RCTIC CRUISE

A

ADMIRAL BYRD

American Admiral Richard E. Byrd's expeditions to Antarctica are some of the seminal adventures of the 20th century. On his first expedition in 1928 Byrd took Hudson's Bay Company Point Blankets along. Much to the Company's delight, the blankets proved more than equal to the task, a fact that the advertising copywriters were happy to exploit.

To the ANTARCTIC with BYRD~

Hudson's Bay Company.
INCORPORATED 2ND MAY 1670.

BYRD ANTARCTIC EXPEDITION
August 11, 1928.

Hudson's Bay Company, Inc.,
165 Broadway,
New York City.

Gentlemen:

We have received our shipment of 72 "point" Hudson's Bay blankets, which we are taking with us to the Antarctic.

Your blanket has been selected as the standard for this Expedition. We realize full well the importance of proper blanket equipment and rely implicitly on the quality of Hudson's Bay Company products.

We appreciate your giving such prompt attention to our order.

Very sincerely yours,

BYRD ANTARCTIC EXPEDITION.

Richard G. Brophy,
Business Manager.

HUDSON'S BAY "POINT" BLANKETS

COLOURS—Camel, Scarlet, Green, Empire Blue, Gray, Khaki, White and Multi-Stripe.

SIZES AND WEIGHTS—

3-Point	3½-Point
60x72 inches	63x81 inches
8 lbs. 5 oz. per pair	10 lbs. per pair

4-Point
72x90 inches
12 lbs. per pair

On sale at all Hudson's Bay Company stores: Winnipeg (Man.), Saskatoon, Yorkton (Sask.), Calgary, Edmonton, Lethbridge (Alta.), Vancouver, Victoria, Kamloops, Nelson and Vernon (B.C.), and at the Company's Fur Trade posts throughout Canada.

G

GRAND FALLS

The annals of Hudson's Bay Company history are full of stories of epic journeys. One lesser known one is that immortalized in the painting *The Discovery of Grand Falls*, 1839, by Walter J. Phillips. The artist captures the exact moment that John McLean, sent to reconnoitre an overland route across Labrador, encountered the magnificent Grand Falls on the Hamilton River. Though the route would prove impractical, McLean's discovery would not. Rechristened Churchill Falls, in 1971 the diverted cataract began to power what is today North America's second-largest hydroelectric dam.

F

FRONTIER

They came from distant lands to work in a remote country. Many were from Scotland—young men who took up positions as apprentice clerks in far-flung Hudson's Bay Company outposts. In this often-lonely frontier, lifelong friendships were forged.

R
REVITALIZATION

Revolving doors welcomed shoppers to Simpsons in downtown Toronto in 1976, as illustrated in this concept drawing.

B

BARBIE

Beginning in 1995 Mattel issued the first in a series of six exclusive HBC-themed collector Barbies to mark the Company's 325th anniversary. *School Spirit Barbie*, dressed in a sporty HBC Point Blanket coat, made her debut in 1996.

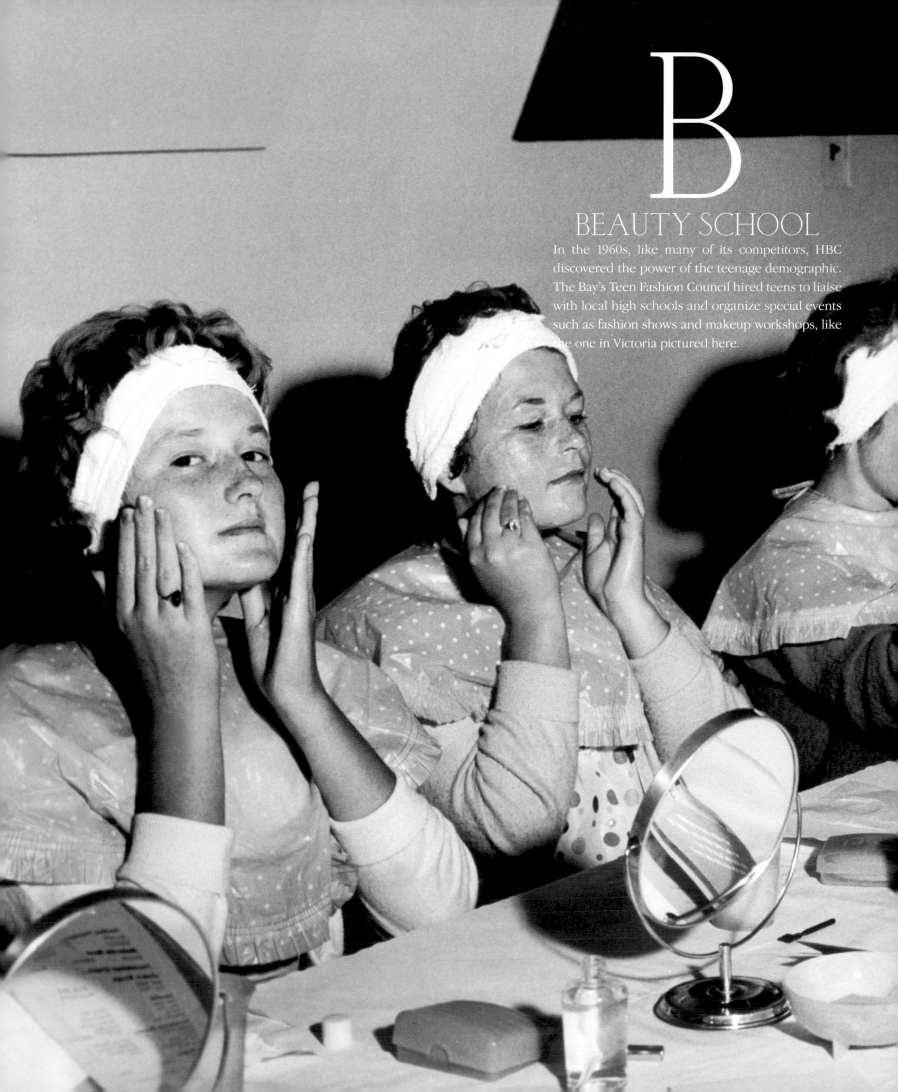

B
BEAUTY SCHOOL

In the 1960s, like many of its competitors, HBC discovered the power of the teenage demographic. The Bay's Teen Fashion Council hired teens to liaise with local high schools and organize special events such as fashion shows and makeup workshops, like the one in Victoria pictured here.

J

JOURNEY

With a historic handshake, two titans of Hudson's Bay Company come face to face in the wilds of British Columbia. In 1828, then Hudson's Bay Company overseas governor George Simpson set out to visit the Company's outpost at Fort Vancouver, in modern Washington State. About halfway through his epic two month journey, he met James Douglas at Fort St. James, B.C. Then a Hudson's Bay Company manager, Douglas would go on to become the Governor of the Crown Colony of British Columbia.

T

TRADITION

In this illustrated letter, famed American frontier painter Charles M. Russell expresses his thanks to Hudson's Bay Company for sending him a history of the Company. It was 1920, and the Company was celebrating its 250th anniversary; it was a time to celebrate the achievements of the past, and to aspire to continuing success in the future.

Sept 5th
1920

Mr Charles H Fair Dear Sir

I am slow thanking you for the Hudson Bay Co history you kindly sent me

I like History and that old fur compenay has made lots of it Thair is hardly a City ore town in your country that did not spring from a Hudson Bay stockade. They were trail brakers of Canada

forty years ago when I came to Montana thair were a fiew Forts in Alberta but no towns

long ago when the Black feet came with robes and sent thair nacked pipe carrier thair were no lady craks with the Hudson Bay But men who new nothing of lace ore lingerie but could tell a cow robe from a bull with thair eyes slint they savyed a gun and thair hands were never fare from one when they traded over the log counter with a black foot

That life has gone and most of the men who lived it but the Hudson Bay still lives in its big stores

Thanking you again for the History

Sincerly yours C M Russell

PRO PELLE

C
COAT OF ARMS

The Hudson's Bay Company coat of arms dates to 1671. A pair of moose supports a shield featuring four beavers, representing the Company's business, and the red Cross of St. George, the national badge of England. A fox, another symbol of the fur trade, sits atop a Cap of Maintenance, which denotes authority. On a ribbon beneath is the Latin motto *Pro Pelle Cutem*, meaning "for the pelt, the skin."

P

PRESERVATION

The Royal Charter of Hudson's Bay Company, five sheets of hand-lettered parchment (animal skin), was granted in 1670 by King Charles II, depicted here on the document's seal. One of the most significant documents in Canadian history, the Charter was scientifically studied and conserved in 1997 before being displayed at Hudson's Bay Company's headquarters, in Toronto.

A
ANNIVERSARY

Dressed in their ceremonial finery, these men have gathered at the stone fort at Lower Fort Garry, north of Winnipeg, to celebrate Hudson's Bay Company's 250th anniversary. The year 1920 marked another major milestone for the venerable Company—it began the process of opening its vast and rich archival holdings to the public.

THE SEAL OF QUALITY
CORPORATED 1670

DRESS STEWART

FABRIC:
Woven in Scotland
from 100% Pure Mohair.

T
TARTAN

While the Hudson's Bay Company Point Blanket does garner the most attention, the Company also has a registered tartan (right). The green, red, yellow and indigo of the multistripe pattern figure prominently in its design. Created in the 1980s, it has appeared on handbags, small leather goods, accessories, and outerwear.

902

740

Red
Fraser

903

CLASSIC

Fine fragrance is now associated with luxury brands, but at the turn of the last century shoppers chose from a variety of scents "on tap" that were decanted into bottles at the point of sale. A handwritten Hudson's Bay Company label recorded the contents.

HUDSON'S BAY CO...
Compagnie de la Bai...
ESTABLISHED 1670 / CONSTI...

CANADA

R
REINVENTION

Combining history and innovative design, 2009 saw the launch of the Hudson's Bay Company Collection. Offering a fresh spin on Hudson's Bay Company's heritage, it takes iconic symbols of Canada and presents them in new and exciting ways. Artisanal maple products producer Ninutik (opposite) and the design team of Smythe—Andrea Lenczner and Christie Smythe, shown here with their version of a Hudson's Bay Company Point Blanket coat—illustrate the concept.

H
HUDSON'S BAY
COMPANY
COLLECTIONS

In recent years, Hudson's Bay Company's proprietary designs have experienced a renaissance, with both reissues from the Company archives and high-profile collaborations with fashion, lifestyle and adventure product designers from around the world.

H

HOLIDAY

For many Canadians going to Hudson's Bay Company to see the annual Christmas windows is a cherished childhood tradition that persists even after they're all grown up. Parents eagerly bring their own children to view modern windows and create their own life-long memories.

S
STARS

Hudson's Bay Company has a long tradition of celebrating celebrity, dating to its earliest days, when the Company gave gifts of beaver hats to men of influence in London. Here, actress Gene Tierney seems pleased by her Hudson's Bay Company Point Blanket, a gift for her role in the 1941 film *Hudson's Bay*.

B
BEAUTY
In a country with one of the world's most diverse populations, The Bay carries at least 2,000 shades of lipstick.

F
FRAGRANCE

Most of the world's top perfume houses are represented in The Bay's fragrance department, which also launches a number of exclusives every season.

T
TOBACCO

Part of Hudson's Bay Company's wholesale line of branded products, in its day Imperial Mixture tobacco, shown here in a 1930 *Beaver* magazine advertisement, was a top seller.

F
FLAG

The historic Hudson's Bay Company flag is essentially the Red Ensign of the British Royal Navy with some modification. Prince Rupert, first Governor of Hudson's Bay Company, was also Vice Admiral of England. By a special warrant dated July 21, 1682, Rupert granted the Company permission to use the modified Ensign at its forts and on its ships entering Hudson Strait. No other private concern was ever granted such a privilege.

FIRST NATIONS

When Canadian artist Doug Levitt was commissioned to paint the 2008 Calgary Stampede poster, he sought inspiration from Canada's most iconic company. Which is why, in *A Man of His People*, a First Nations chief in full headdress carries a pennant made from a Hudson's Bay Company Point Blanket as he rides amid the splendour of the Rockies.

T
TRADING CEREMONY

While First Nations traders might arrive at the posts on Hudson Bay at any time during the spring and summer months, June and July saw the majority of activity. Their arrival was one of the high points of the year and, as such, was met with a great deal of pomp and circumstance. *The Trading Ceremony at York Factory, 1780s,* by Adam Sherriff Scott, is based on contemporary accounts of the ceremonies that took place.

E
ELIZABETH

From the very beginning, Hudson's Bay Company's royal connections have helped shape its destiny. From the days of King Charles II and Prince Rupert to royal visits to Canada from the reigning queen, Elizabeth II, the Honourable Company has a storied and regal history.

D

DEDICATION

The sign says it all—despite chest-deep
snow from a Saskatoon blizzard, there's
no way this little tyke was going to miss
the great deals to be had during 1967's
"Bay Day" sale.

F

FLAGSHIP

After 1910 Hudson's Bay Company decided to concentrate on its retail business. As a result the Company invested in a major expansion program for its urban stores across the west. The result was a series of state of the art retail palaces in Winnipeg, Saskatoon, Edmonton, Calgary, Vancouver and Victoria. The Calgary store, depicted here, was the first of the "original six" to open, in 1913.

T
TERCENTENNIAL

Hudson's Bay Company's three hundredth anniversary, in 1970, was a groovy affair, if this illustration is any indication. The oldest company in North America, Hudson's Bay Company has celebrated its anniversaries in numerous ways: publishing commemorative medals and books, launching a magazine, *The Beaver*, in 1920, and commissioning a replica of its famous flagship, the *Nonsuch*, for its tercentennial.

F
FACTORY

The earliest Hudson's Bay Company Point Blankets were made in factories in Oxfordshire, England. In the 1800s, Hudson's Bay Company expanded its operations to Yorkshire mills. Today, all Point Blankets are made in Yorkshire, near Leeds.

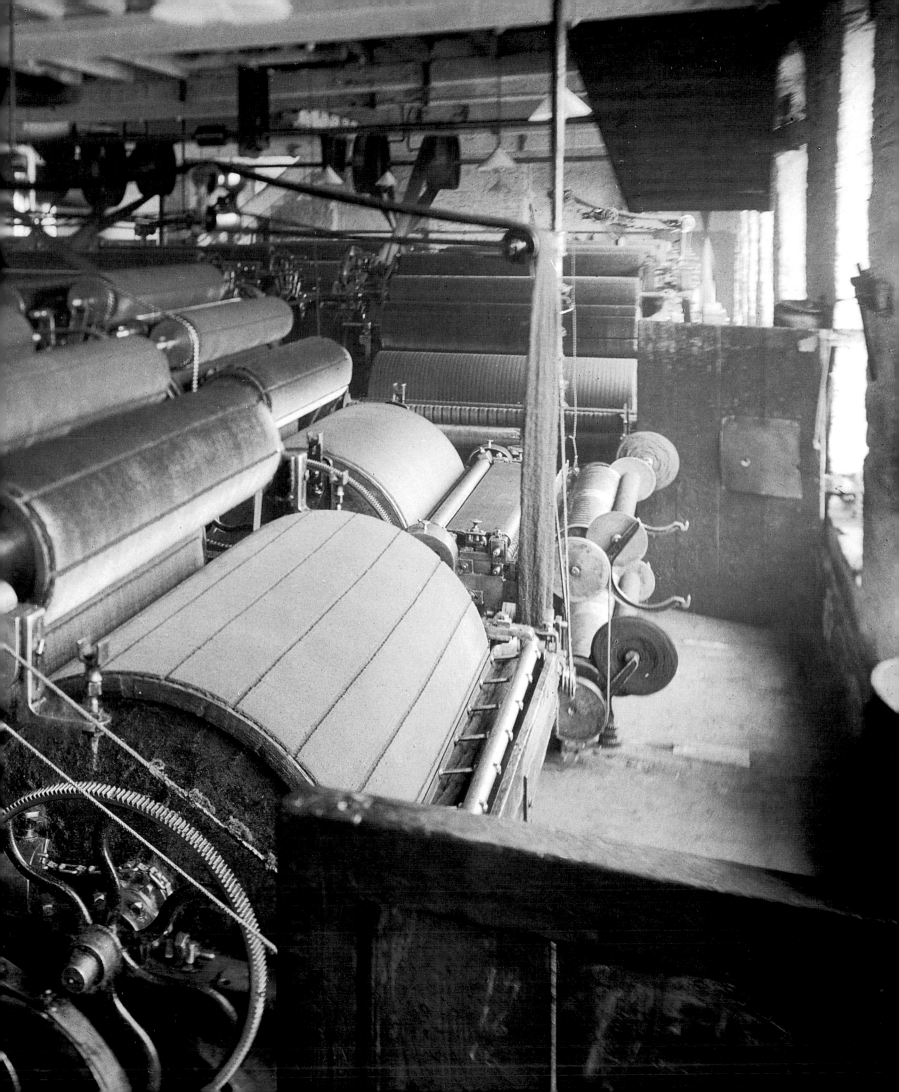

B
BUSINESS

Ralph Parsons at his desk in the St. Lawrence/Labrador District Office in the 1920s. Thanks to his role in developing posts in the Arctic, particularly on Baffin Island, Parsons earned the nickname "The King of Baffin Land." In 1931 he was named Fur Trade Commissioner, a post he held until his retirement in 1940.

PRIVATE BRANDS

Private or house brands are created specifically for a retailer's target customers. They help cement the relationship between the two and build customer loyalty. Most often seen in clothing and housewares, Hudson's Bay Company private brands have, in the past, been developed for foodstuffs, furniture and generic drugs, as this c. 1937 image of the in-store pharmacy in Winnipeg clearly shows.

M
MAKING
HISTORY

For many Canadians Hudson's Bay Company is a family affair. When Jessica Weirmier and Nicoli Garner were married at Quebec's Hôtel de Glace (Ice Hotel) in February 2005 they wore Hudson's Bay Company Point Blanket capotes they made themselves and travelled by dog-sled to the ceremony. Hudson's Bay Company had special meaning for Jessica: her grandparents met and fell in love when both were working for the Company in Victoria, B.C., in the 1940s.

Q

QUALITY

First trademarked in 1914, the Seal of Quality is most closely associated with Hudson's Bay Point Blankets, and appears on all blanket labels. Since then the Seal of Quality has also been used for other premium products.

S

SACRIFICE

When war erupted in Europe in 1939, Canada's department stores and their staff did their part, whether it was by serving on the front lines, as support staff for the military, or by organizing sales drives for Victory Bonds.

B. Hall
Grocery
March 30/42
Returned to Grocery. May - 1945.

Sept. THE *Bayonet* 1945

VOLUME 10　　　　　　　　　　　　　　　　　　　　NO. 4

WELCOME

GENERAL SERVICE

HOME

SAILORS • SOLDIERS • AIRMEN

WRENS • CWACS • RCAF-WD

A

ART

From 1913 to 1970 Hudson's Bay Company commissioned a series of artworks for use on its annual calendar. Depicting events drawn from the Company's history, such as *First White Women Arrive at Moose Fort, 1683*, by Will Davies, the resulting paintings form one of the pillars of the Hudson's Bay Company's corporate art collection.

FORT ALBANY

One of three original Hudson's Bay Company outposts built in the late 1600s on James Bay, Fort Albany, in Ontario, was a thorn in the side of the rival French fur merchants in Montreal. Hudson's Bay Company's strategy was based on building forts at the mouths of all major rivers leading into Hudson Bay.

N
NORTH WEST COMPANY

A bitter rival that became a business partner, the North West Company was founded by Montreal merchants who sought to defeat Hudson's Bay Company and dominate the fur trade. After years of intense competition that gave way to bloodshed, the two companies merged under the Hudson's Bay Company banner in 1821.

F

FORT
QU'APPELLE

Fort Qu'Appelle, established in 1801 in modern day Saskatchewan, was one of an ever expanding trade network of forts and outposts that helped to open the continent. Many forts became the heart of major Canadian towns and cities. Note the fort's wooden palisade and centralized plan.

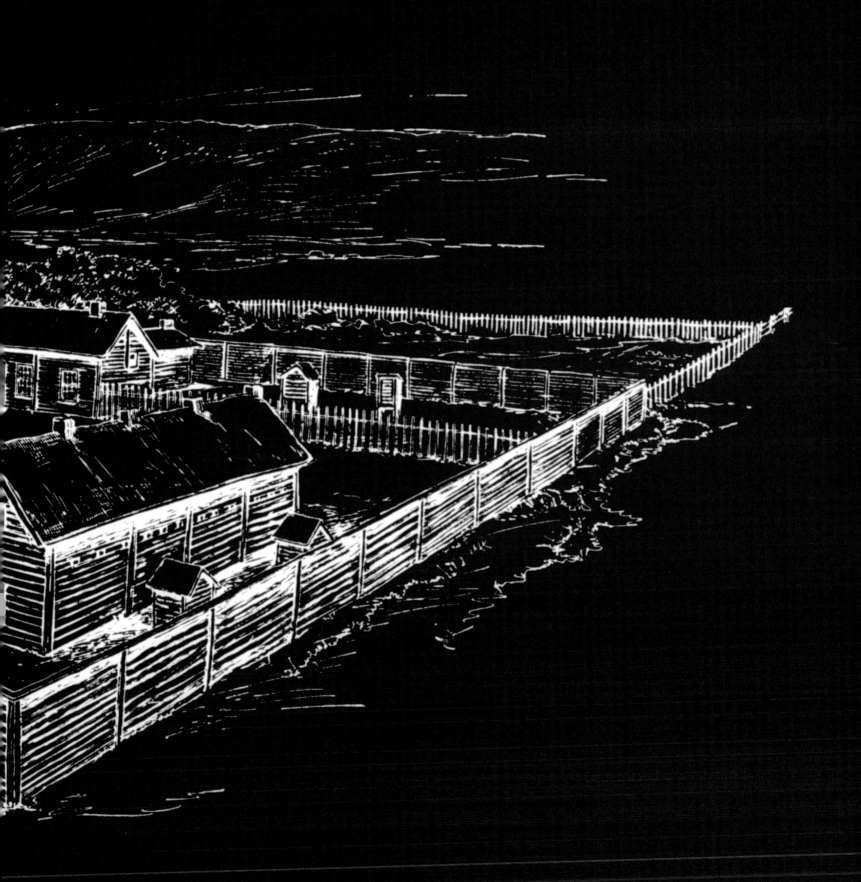

pelle in 1867.

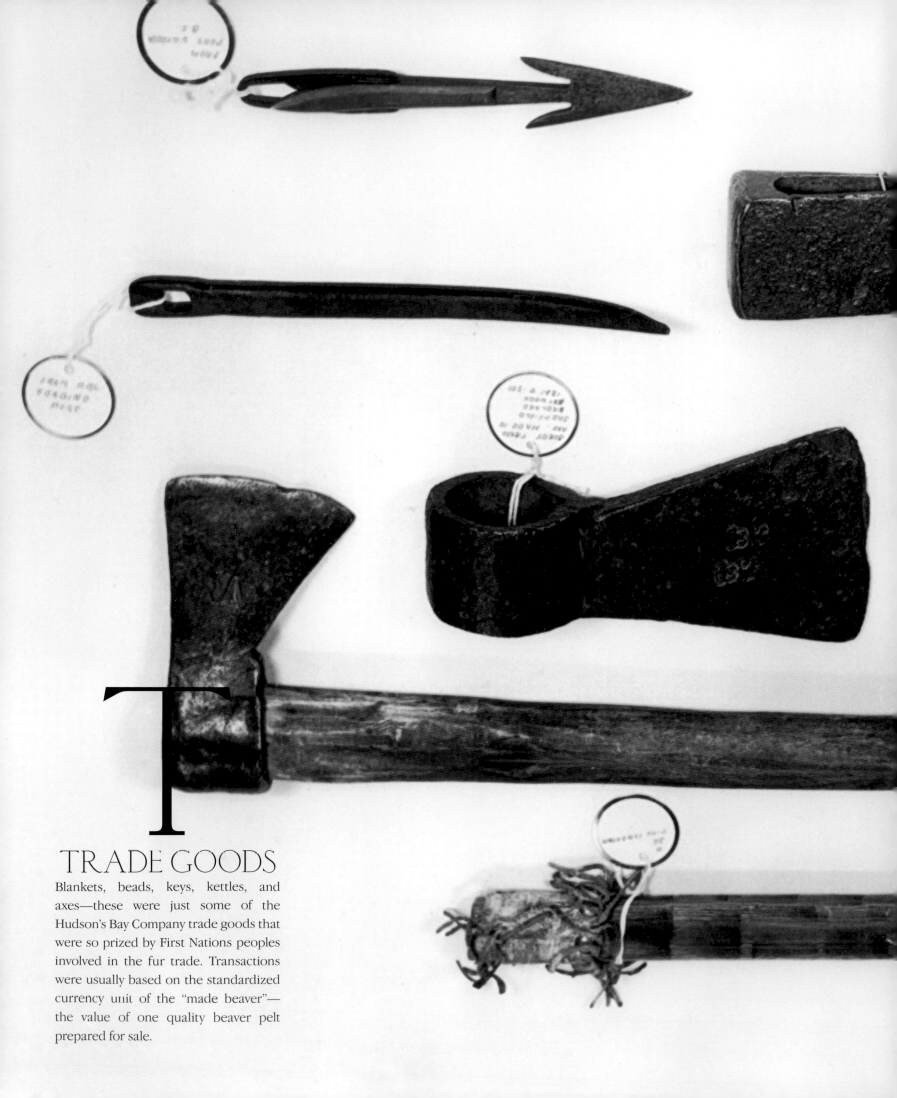

T

TRADE GOODS

Blankets, beads, keys, kettles, and axes—these were just some of the Hudson's Bay Company trade goods that were so prized by First Nations peoples involved in the fur trade. Transactions were usually based on the standardized currency unit of the "made beaver"— the value of one quality beaver pelt prepared for sale.

I
INUIT ART

With the care of a true craftsman, Seeguapik of Povungnetuk trims between the arm and the face of a soapstone sculpture in 1956 (opposite). A strong advocate for Inuit artists, in 1953 Hudson's Bay Company became the sole provider of Inuit art to the Canadian Handicrafts Guild and opened its own marketing division for the art in 1979.

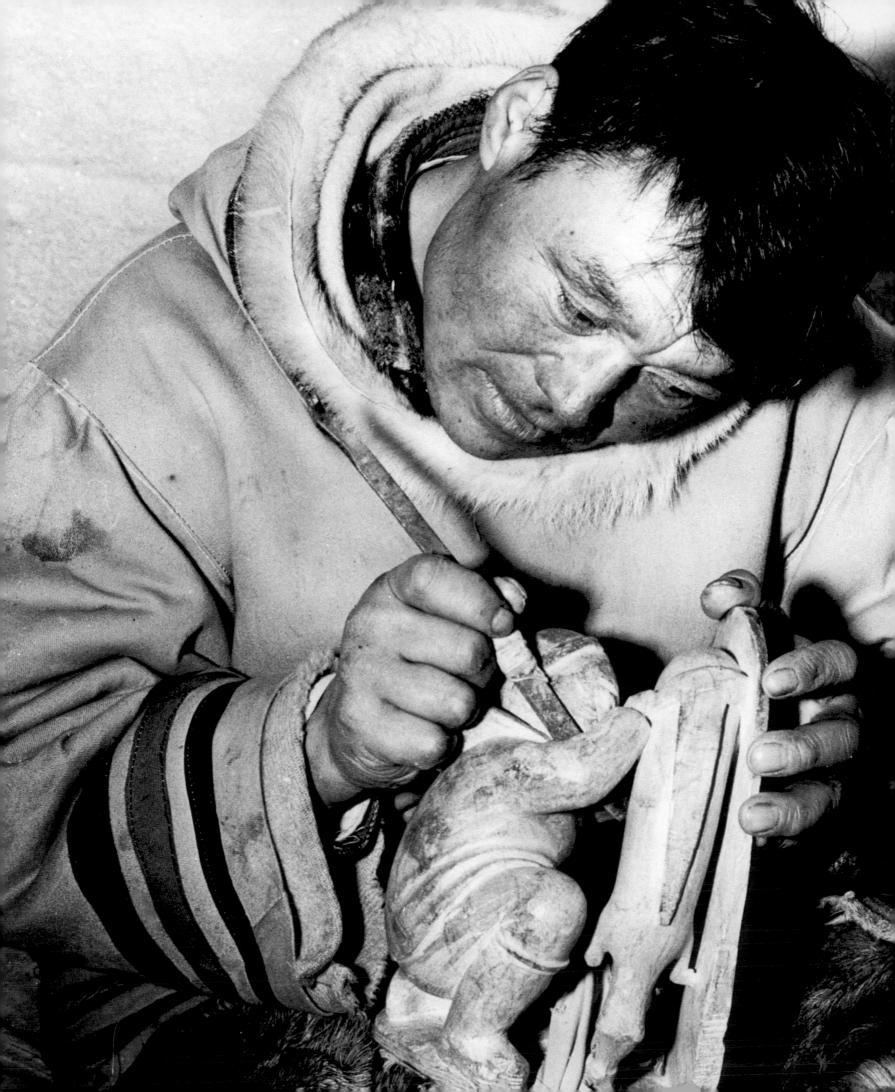

S
SHIPPING

As a British company operating overseas, Hudson's Bay Company necessarily became expert in the business of shipping. Centuries of transatlantic crossings were supplemented by North American based fleets that operated along the coasts, on the larger northern rivers and into the Arctic Ocean. Such work was not without risk. Ships were often turned back by fierce weather and impenetrable ice. And from time to time ships were lost, most, like the *Lady Kindersley*, caught and eventually crushed by the Arctic ice pack.

D
DOGSLED

Travel by dogsled was the preferred method of covering long distances in the winter, when lakes and rivers were conveniently frozen. Traders kept their own teams and lavished them with care and attention. This painting, *Last Dog Train Leaving Fort Garry, 1909*, by Charles Comfort, captures some of the colour of a train of sleds setting out. Ribbons and bells on the dogs were not simply ornamental; in blizzard conditions they helped locate valuable animals that otherwise might be lost.

M
MERCHANT

A Hudson's Bay Company man inspects furs presented by a trapper, Archie White, in order to determine their value—a scene repeated on countless occasions throughout Hudson's Bay Company's history. For almost 250 years, the fur trade was the lifeblood of the Company. But as demand for fur waned, trading posts were gradually transformed into Company stores. Hudson's Bay Company exited the fur business in 1987.

R

RECRUITS

For centuries Hudson's Bay Company vessels brought a new intake of apprentice clerks to North America each summer. Young British men—like the class of 1928, pictured here—signed multi-year contracts to work in the Fur Trade. The last such transatlantic voyage took place in 1964.

Picnic
COOLER
MADE IN CANADA FOR
Hudson's Bay Company.
INCORPORATED 2ND MAY 1670

PRO PELLE CUTEM

C
COOLER

Over the years the Company developed an extensive program of private brand merchandise. Like explorers from the past, modern families could rely on HBC to outfit them for their personal adventures with items such as this picnic cooler, c. 1966.

C

CHRISTMAS

Everyone's favourite holiday is crunch time for most retailers, who typically make or miss their annual goals during the short holiday season. While shoppers marvel at animated window displays like this 1959 Simpsons scene, retailers hope the items they've chosen will end up under the tree.

A
AVIATION

When the Company's first aircraft was acquired in 1939, it was used primarily to transport executives. As business increased, especially in the remote North, air travel would serve as a lifeline across the Company's far-reaching territory, securing freight contracts with such airlines as Canadian Pacific.

Hudson's Bay Company Archives, Archives of Manitoba (1987/363-L-49/20). Photograph by C.N. Stephen.

C
CREATIVITY

The modern Hudson's Bay Company is a launching pad for emerging fashion designers and a Canadian source for trendsetters from around the world. Recent infusions of new blood include British designer Mary Kantrantzou and American Jason Wu (this page).

A
ADVERTISING

Successful advertising aims to create a feeling as much as it does a desire for any particular product. This advertisement from 1937 emphasizes Hudson's Bay Company's long association with the great Canadian outdoors. We see rugged men relaxing in the landscape along with a cherished pet— and almost overlook the clothing, Hudson's Bay Company Point Blanket and Imperial Mixture that accompany them.

E
EVENTS

Sarah Jessica Parker cuts a stunning figure in a Marchesa tuxedo jacket and a Halston bandage dress. The *Sex and the City* star was in Toronto in March 2010 to launch Halston Heritage at The Bay—just one of Hudson's Bay's signature events where celebrity and shopping intersect.

S
SHOES

As shoes have become the new It bags, The Room has become a fashionista's destination for designs by the likes of Alaïa and Brian Atwood.

F

FUR

Originally the fur trade sought beaver pelts as raw material for felt for the hat-making industry. By the late 19th century the introduction of silk hats had eroded this market. But soon an emerging middle class with an appetite for premium goods saw fur transformed into a luxury fashion item.

M
MODELS

Beautiful women wearing beautiful clothes inspire us all. And the great news is that many of today's top models are Canadians. Consequently, The Bay is delighted to feature homegrown talent as much as possible, such as Jessica Stam (this page) and Daria Werbowy (opposite).

S

SOCIETY

With their flowing gowns, silk gloves, and stylish shawls, these mannequins at Simpsons' St. Regis Room evoke a scene from a courtly ball. With the most exclusive and carefully edited selection of evening wear, Hudson's Bay Company has always been synonymous with timeless elegance and high style.

T

TEDDY BEAR

Say hello to Pelly, a Hudson's Bay Company "heritage" bear named after Sir John Henry Pelly, the Company's seventeenth Governor. Starting in 1985, Hudson's Bay Company began selling teddy bears at Christmas to raise funds for charity. Each bear is named after a person of historic significance to the Company.

B

BAYMAN

Look up at the sky. It's a bird. It's a plane. No, wait . . . it's Bayman — the scourge of high prices everywhere! Introduced in the 1970s, the Company's cheeky crusader fought an ongoing fashion war against his nemesis, Flash Eaton, who represented the rival Eaton's chain.

N

NASCOPIE

The most celebrated steamship in the Hudson's Bay Company fleet, the RMS *Nascopie* plied the northern waters of Canada for more than three decades. Beginning in 1912 she carried supplies and passengers to remote Hudson's Bay Company outposts every year. The ship, which takes its name from First Nations people in Quebec and Labrador, sank in 1947 in modern Nunavut.

C

CISCO KID

In 1958, the Cisco Kid and his trusty compadre, Black Jack, were guests of honour at the Calgary Stampede. While there, the television stars received Hudson's Bay Company Point Blankets, the national gift of choice to distinguished visitors. There's no word on whether the heroic Mexican caballeros converted their blankets into ponchos.

N
NORTHWEST PASSAGE

As noted in the Royal Charter of 1670, the Company had "undertaken an Expedition for Hudson's Bay in the North-west Part of America, for the Discovery of a new Passage into the South Sea." It's clear that for the Crown, at least, the "finding of some trade for Furs, Minerals and other considerable Commodities" was of secondary importance. For the next two centuries exploration of the Arctic allowed the Company to pursue both goals.

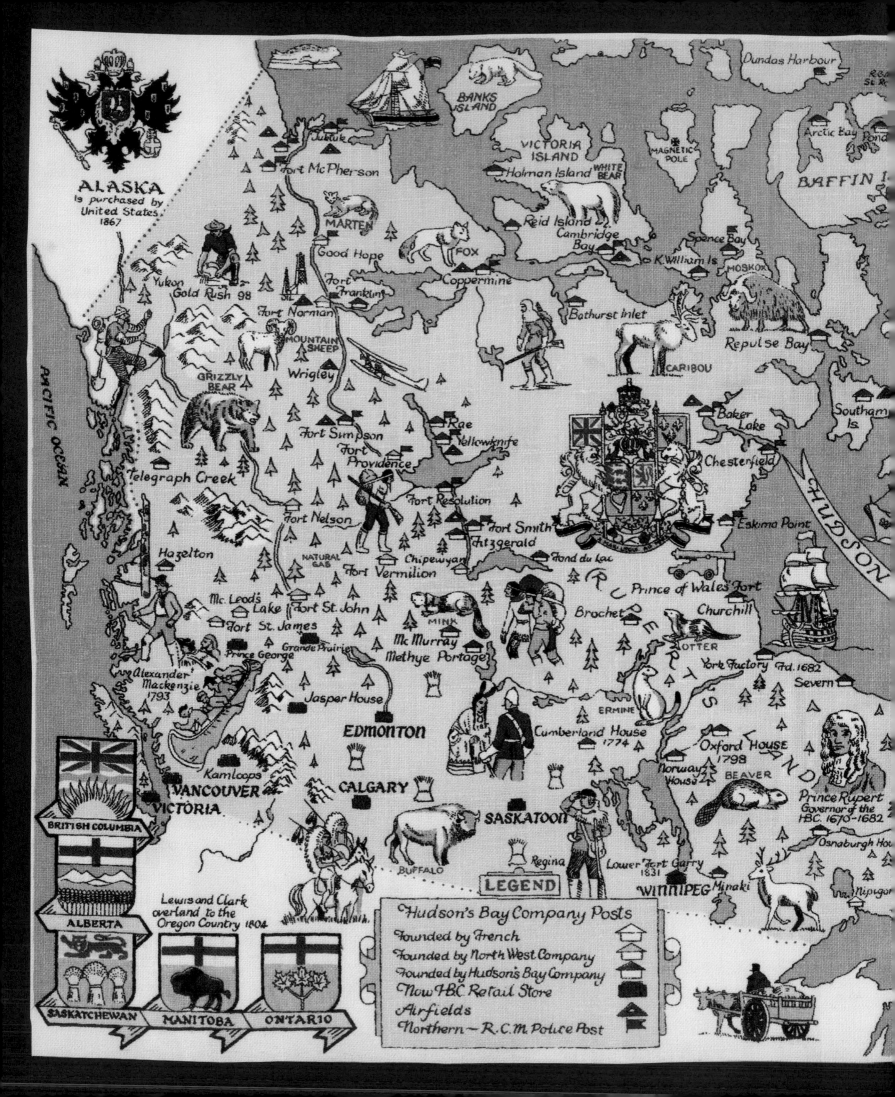

S

SEA TO SEA ... TO SEA

It was the sea route via Hudson Bay that underpinned Hudson's Bay Company's successful business model and allowed it to achieve supremacy in the fur trade. At its height the Company occupied more than half a continent from the Atlantic to the Pacific and north to the Arctic Ocean, as this map from the mid 1950s clearly illustrates.

CHARLES II

Contrary to popular belief, the Hudson's Bay Company Royal Charter wasn't actually "signed" by King Charles II. Instead, it was affixed with his royal seal. The Charter, dated May 2, 1670, granted the Hudson's Bay Company a monopoly over Rupert's Land, an area of nearly 4 million square kilometres—about 40% of modern Canada.

M
MUSES

In fall 2010, fashion designers from the U.K. flew to Toronto for God Save The Queen, a gala tribute to new British style. The designers posed with their muses for an HBC fashion shoot (shown: Charlotte Olympia with stylist Valentine Fillol-Cordier).

R
ROYALTY

When Princess Elizabeth and Prince Philip toured Canada in October 1951, they kept warm thanks to Hudson's Bay Company's iconic Point Blanket. Founded in London in 1670, the Company's head office remained on the other side of the Atlantic until 1970. A Canadian company today, Hudson's Bay Company's ties to England are many.

Spring and Summer
1941 · No. 88

WOODWARDS

WOODWARD'S

With their rosy cheeks and gaily-coloured skirts, these girls from a 1951 Woodward's catalogue epitomize the moxie of the times. Established in 1892 in British Columbia, the Woodward's chain was purchased a century later by Hudson's Bay Company.

R
RONALD SEARLE

Filled with festive fun, Hudson's Bay Company celebrated its three hundredth anniversary in 1970 by hiring illustrator Ronald Searle to create a series of drawings—including this cover image—for a lighthearted history of the Company, entitled *The Great Fur Opera*.

Castor du Canada

I
ICONS

The world knows Canada through its icons: The maple leaf. The canoe. Hockey. Thanks to the fur trade—and Hudson's Bay Company—the humble, hardworking beaver has also become a symbol of Canada.

F
FORT

The nexus of the fur trade, Hudson's Bay Company forts were centres of commerce and community life. The explorer David Thompson used the fort at Alberta's Rocky Mountain House as a base as he travelled the Rockies in the early 1800s.

G

GOVERNORS

For more than 340 years, the Governors of the Honourable Company have steered it through all manner of challenges. To date, thirty-nine people—thirty-eight men and one woman—have held the title, including John, Lord Churchill, 1st Duke of Marlborough (opposite), and Donald Smith, Baron Strathcona and Mount Royal (this page).

I
INUIT

Without the Inuit people of the Far North and the First Nations peoples from across Canada, the Hudson's Bay Company simply could not have flourished. From the aboriginal peoples early Hudson's Bay Company traders learned to survive and adapt to the harsh Canadian climate. They also acted as guides in the vast wilderness and were essential partners in the success of the fur trade.

U
UNIFORMS

The 1964 Canadian Winter Olympic skating team (this page) show off their Hudson's Bay Company Point Blanket coats in this casual shot from the Innsbruck Winter Games. Contestants for the title of Winter Queen in The Pas, northern Manitoba (opposite), are ready for whatever the weather may throw at them, thanks to their cozy attire.

C

CAPOTE

In 1903 Bear Chief cuts a proud figure in his traditional capote—a wrap coat made from a Hudson's Bay Company blanket. A common garment among the First Nations, many, many versions of the capote were made, and variations in style were common: with or without hood, embroidered, beaded or with leather fringing. Easy to make, warm and water-repellent, the capote was made for the Canadian climate.

SPORTS

No fouls here! The Hudson's Bay Company "Fur Trappers" was the best ladies basketball team in the Alberta mercantile league in 1924 (opposite). Beginning in 1920, Hudson's Bay Company jumped aboard the fitness fad, building staff tennis courts and sponsoring in-house sports teams.

KATE McCREA - CENTRE & CAPT.

JOE SPRINGER - COACH

JEAN ROBERTSON - FORWARD

Hudson's Bay BasketBall Team
The "FUR TRAPPERS"
1924

ETHELEEN McEWEN - CENTRE

VIOLET DAVIS - FORWARD

LILLIAN SAUNDERS - GUARD

BOTTLED IN SCOTLAND

The Governor and Company of Adventurers  of England Trading into Hudson's Bay

INCORPORATED — 2ND MAY 1670 —

HUDSON'S BAY

Best Procurable

SCOTCH WHISKY

Finest old Scotch Whisky
Distilled Blended and Bottled in Scotland

Hudson's Bay Company

EDINBURGH, SCOTLAND.

CONTENTS **25** OUNCES

L
LIQUOR

The quintessential combination of fire and ice, Hudson's Bay Company scotch (on the rocks, of course) became an instant classic starting in 1923. The Company entered the wholesale market in 1907 due to the growing demand for both liquor and groceries in the expanding West.

J

JOSHUA TREE

In 1969, Rolling Stone Keith Richards and his girlfriend, model Anita Pallenberg, accompanied Byrds guitarist Gram Parsons to his favourite place: the desert at Joshua Tree National Park, in California. The legendary trip, immortalized in photos by Michael Cooper, was a lost weekend of mythic proportions that came to symbolize an era. Anita warded off the chill of the desert night in a Hudson's Bay Company Point Blanket coat

S
SERVICE

In 1952, customers of the Hat Bar at the Company's Winnipeg store could make their selection from a wide assortment of merchandise. More than simply pushing product, retail relies on a keen understanding of the client's needs, aspirations, interests and lives. The more a retailer understands the customer the stronger the relationship between them. Meeting customer needs with diverse product offerings and personal service yields the ultimate retail commodity: customer loyalty.

CORPORATE CITIZENSHIP

It only makes sense for a company like Hudson's Bay Company to be engaged in the communities where it does business. For decades that support has taken many forms, from promoting local theatre to selling "heritage" bears to raising money for charity.

Canvas Covered Canoes

PETERBOROUGHS

"Prospector" Canoes

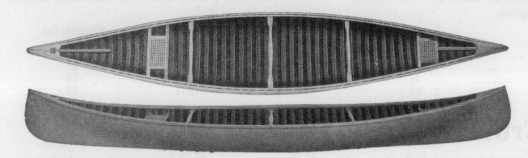

Model Number	Code Word	Length, feet	Beam, inches	Depth, inches		Average Cap., lbs.
89X	POND	14	34	13	60	600
90X	STREAM	15	35	13½	70	650
92X	RIVER	16	36	14	75	850
66X	BUSH	17	37	14½	85	950
68X	PORTAGE	18	38	15	90	1100

Shoe Keel ½-inch thick, 2½ inches wide, $3.00 extra.   Extra Depth, $3.00 per inch.

"Freight" Canoes

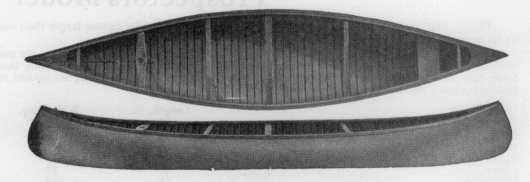

Strength and carrying capacity are requisite features on this type of canoe. The ribs and planking are heavier than on smaller canoes. Cedar is used entirely for these parts. The canvas is also heavier. They have hardwood bars, also mast thwart and step for sail. They are painted inside and out.

Model Number	Code Word	Length, feet	Beam, inches	Depth, inches	Weight, lbs.	Average Cap., lbs.
566	MARTIN	17	42	17	120	1600
68XX	BIRCH	18	42	18	130	1600
69XX	SPRUCE	19	44	19	150	1800
572	BEAVER	20	54	20	190	2800
576	LAC SEUL	22	62	24	290	5000
670	THICKET	18	50	20	150	1800
671	PELICAN	19	51	21	160	2000

Canoes Nos. 670, 671 and 572 do not tumble in on the sides like other canoes.   The sides are straight or flare out, making them drier in rough water.

Heavy shoe keel is standard equipment.   When further protection is required on the bottom, bilge or rub keels can be put on at an extra cost of $3.00 for each keel.

"Prospector" and "Freight" Models with Square Stern

For use with outboard motors, we build some of the "Prospector" and "Freight" canoes with square or "V" shaped stern which does not interfere with their paddling qualities.

The capacity is the same as the corresponding sizes in the "Prospector" and "Freight" list.

Code Word	Length, feet	Beam, inches	Depth, inches	Weight, lbs.
TRAVELLER	17	37	14½	95
NAVIGATOR	18	38	15	100
TRANSPORT	18	42	18	135

ARCADIAN COVRT

A
ARCADIAN COURT

Since its grand opening, in 1929, this jewel of
Art Deco design has been known as the place
"where Toronto does lunch." The restaurant and
event space at the flagship Queen Street location
has hosted the luminaries of fashion, politics, and
the arts and was, in 1967, the site of Sotheby's first-
ever auction outside Britain.

as served to the
Company's Officers
since 1701

TURN TO OPEN

The Governor and Company of Adventurers
of England Trading into Hudson's Bay

INCORPORATED 2ND MAY 1670

HUDSON'S BAY
BRAND
Best Procurable
BLENDED SCOTCH WHISKY
100% SCOTCH WHISKIES
Produce of and Bottled in Scotland by
Hudson's Bay Company
EDINBURGH, SCOTLAND.
86·8° PROOF   REG. U.S. PAT. OFF.   4/5 QUART

IMPORTED BY
Hudson's Bay Company, Inc.
NEW YORK, N.Y.

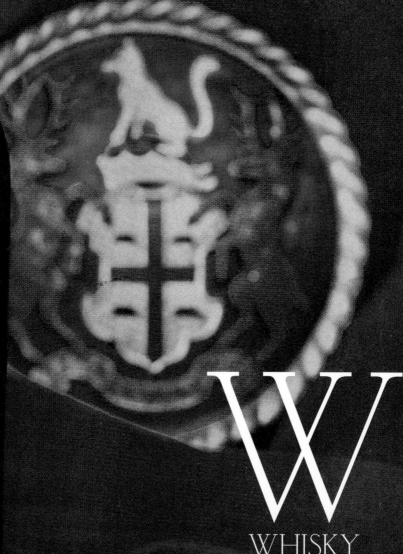

W

WHISKY

Hudson's Bay Company's "Best Procurable" brand of
premium scotch, introduced in 1923, was one of the
Company's top liquors. Distilled in Edinburgh,
Scotland, the blended, 86 proof whisky certainly
kept its connoisseurs in high spirits.

G

GRAPHIC

Instantly recognizable, Hudson's Bay Company's original Gothic-style script is unique: it's based on no known font and had to be hand-duplicated. In 1965, when Hudson's Bay Company launched its new brand, The Bay, the New York firm Lippincott & Margulies updated the script. Today, the so-called "ribbon" B is one of the most recognized symbols in Canada.

the Bay

F
FOOD

Over the years, Hudson's Bay Company has had a hand in almost every kind of comestible imaginable, from catering to confectionary. Each of the original six flagship stores had elegant dining rooms and also offered food for sale.

BAKERY SPECIALTIES WEDDING CAKES

Z
ZELLERS

Founded in 1931, the Zellers chain was acquired by Hudson's Bay Company in 1978. In the early years it was known for quality. In 2011 the Company announced the sale of the majority of Zellers store leases to Target.

ELER'S LIMITED

RIFTY CANADIANS

"ZELLER'S"

M
MORGAN'S

A Montreal institution since 1845, when Morgan's opened a store on Ste. Catherine St. in 1891 the retail industry promptly shifted to that part of the city. Hudson's Bay Company's 1960 acquisition of Morgan's ten-store chain brought the Company to the Montreal, Ottawa and Toronto markets.

S
THE ROBERT SIMPSON CO.

Toronto's leading ladies display the latest in turn-of-the-century fashion in this 1899 Simpson catalogue. Hudson's Bay Company purchased the Simpson chain in 1978, eventually converting its locations —including the flagship store in Toronto—to The Bay.

J
JAVA

Nothing perked Canadians up like a hot cup of Hudson's Bay Company brand coffee or tea. Under the watchful eyes of factory staff, shipments of the precious, caffeinated cargo are vacuum-sealed in Vancouver in 1945.

D
DELIVERY

Home-delivery service was a key component of the success of Hudson's Bay Company's retail operations, then and now. Teams of horses and wagons gave way to fleets of delivery trucks, like this one from 1932. Today, home-delivery and messenger service continues to be yet another example of Hudson's Bay Company's devotion to its clients.

S
SALMON

Natural abundance spawned a lucrative new industry for Hudson's Bay Company starting in the 1830s, in British Columbia, and later, in Newfoundland. Purchasers from as far away as London, Australia, and Hawaii prized the quality of the Company's Hubay and Labdor brands.

L
LINGERIE

From garters to girdles, Hudson's Bay Company's lingerie department in Winnipeg, Manitoba, offered customers of the 1930s the latest in ladies' dainties. Some things never change.

THE 'BAY' BROADCAST

LISTEN TO THE
'SHOPPING HOSTESS'

ON THE AIR

\$7.95

FEATURED
ON THE AIR
TODAY

STUDIO

DAILY AT
.45 – 11.15 A.M

CORY 2 HEAT STOVES
$535

B

BROADCAST

What better way to make waves than by taking to the airwaves? Launched on May 2, 1922, CFAC radio station in Calgary, Alberta, broadcast from the city's flagship Hudson's Bay Company store. The station kept customers tuned-in to the latest news, sports, and weather—as well as Hudson's Bay Company fashions.

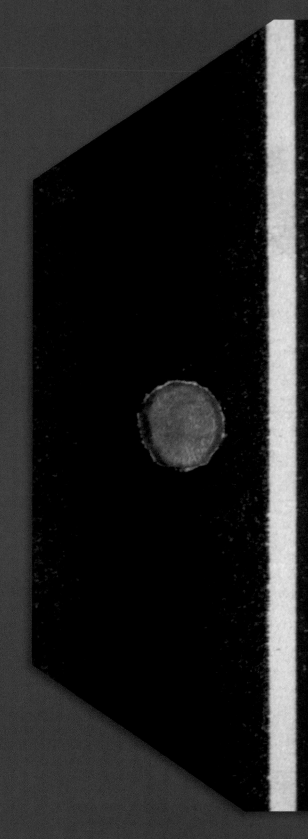

A GENUINE
BUM

FORT O

"making fr

ENGLISH AIRTITE
ER BARREL

ontaining

ARRY TEA

ends everywhere"

lb. Net

F
FORT GARRY

As this 1930 tag attests, friendships were often cemented over a cup of Hudson's Bay Company brand Fort Garry Tea. It was named for a pair of Manitoba forts—Upper Fort Garry, at the Forks in modern-day Winnipeg, and Lower Fort Garry, located some forty-five kilometres downstream—that played key roles in the fur trade.

L
LAND

As twin rails of steel crossed the
continent, thousands of settlers followed.
Waiting for them, with the supplies they
needed to survive and thrive in the
harsh Western frontier, was Hudson's
Bay Company. It also sold thousands
of new homesteads through its Land
Department, which closed in 1961.

Hudson's Bay Vending

A division of HUDSON'S BAY COMPANY

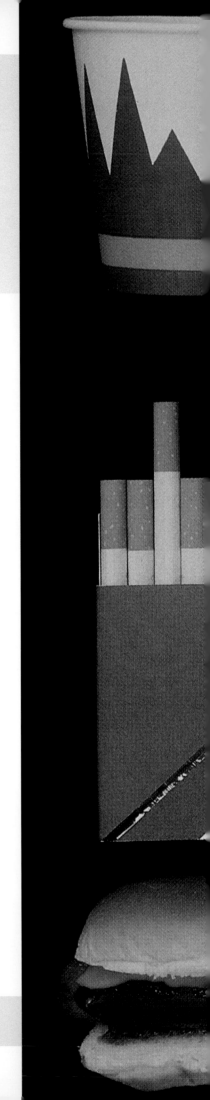

V

VENDING

The early 1900s saw Hudson's Bay Company expand into wholesale, offering lines of Hudson's Bay Company-branded tea, tobacco, liquor, and other goods. In the 1970s, it introduced what was then the cutting edge of convenience—vending machines.

Canada's only national vending service company.

S
STYLE

Over the last few years, the company has produced a series of high-end look books in collaboration with top fashion photographers, models and stylists. In this image from the spring/summer 2011 campaign for The Room, models Jessica Stam and Jacquelyn Jablonski pose for photographer Jason Kibbler.

NOV '09

FAS ON

LOOK HOT FOR LESS

CASHMERE, LEATHER, EVEN JIMMY CHOOS!

BEST BEAUTY BUYS UNDER $25

TWILIGHT'S NEWEST STAR **NOOT SEEAR**

HOW TO DO THE '80S RIGHT
THE SHAPES, THE COLOURS, THE JEWELLERY

QUIT SMOKING AND LOSE WEIGHT YES, YOU CAN!

Kick your fear of laser eye surgery

M
MULTISTRIPE

The multistripe pattern of four stripes in green, red, yellow, and indigo, is synonymous with Hudson's Bay Company. It is instantly recognized worldwide, so much so that these colours connote Canada itself. Lifted straight from the famous Hudson's Bay Company Point Blanket, which introduced the pattern around 1800, the multistripe has adorned everything from linens to clothes to housewares. Since 2009 it has been an integral part of the Company's corporate visual identity.

M
MONTREAL

La belle ville is internationally renowned for its street-meets-chic style. This cosmopolitan city's connection to Hudson's Bay Company dates back centuries, to the earliest days of the fur trade, and continues today as the site of one of its major department stores.

W
WARM

When you're the coldest country on earth, staying warm is a major preoccupation. One way to keep spirits high is to carry a Hudson's Bay Company flask.

To all to whom

These Presents s...
Governor and Company of...
Send Greeting Whereas the
said name of "The Governor and Company
by His late Majesty King Charles the Second
the said Company and their Successors the

in whatsoever latitude they should be that lay within the entrance of the Straits commonly called Hudson
Confines of the Seas bays lakes rivers creeks and sounds aforesaid that were not already actually possessed by
other Christian Prince or State and that the said land should be from thenceforth reckoned and reputed
and whereby His said Majesty made and constituted the said Governor and Company and their successors
and of all other the premises saving the faith allegiance and sovereign Dominion due to his said Majesty his
their Successors such rights of Government and other rights privileges liberties franchises powers and authorities in
said Letters Patent the said Governor and Company have exercised and enjoyed the sole right thereby gra...
enjoyed other rights privileges liberties franchises powers and authorities thereby granted And the said Go...
parts of British North America not forming part of Ruperts Land or of Canada or of British Columbia
other things) enacted that it shall be lawful for Her present Majesty Queen Victoria by and with
Houses of Parliament of Canada to admit Ruperts Land and the North Western Territory or either
conditions as are in the Address expressed and as Her Majesty thinks fit to approve subject to t...
Land Act 1868 it is enacted (amongst other things) That for the purposes of that Act the ...
held or claimed to be held by the said Governor and Company and that it shall be competen...
Her Majesty by any Instrument under Her Sign Manual and Signet to accept a Surrender of all o...
powers and authorities whatsoever granted or purported to be granted by the said Letters
upon such terms and conditions as shall be agreed upon by and between Her Majesty...
Surrender shall not be accepted by Her Majesty until the terms and conditions upon which Ru...
have been approved of by Her Majesty and embodied in an Address to Her Majesty from the ...
of the British North America Act 1867 And that upon the acceptance by Her Majesty of ...
and all other privileges liberties franchises powers and authorities whatsoever granted or...
Governor and Company within Ruperts Land and which shall have been so surrendered shall
contained shall prevent the said Governor and Company from continuing to carry on in Rup...
said Majesty Queen Victoria and the said Governor and Company have agreed to terms an...
surrender to Her said Majesty pursuant to the provision in that behalf in the Ruperts La...
rights privileges liberties franchises powers and authorities and all the lands and territorie...
or mentioned) granted or purported to be granted by the said Letters Patent and also all s...
Governor and Company in any parts of British North America not forming part of Rup...
the intent that after such surrender has been effected and accepted under the provision...
into the Union of the Dominion of Canada pursuant to the herein before mentioned Acts
on which it has been agreed that the said Surrender is to be made by the said Gove...
the Company) to Her said Majesty are as follows (that is to say);———

First. The Canadian Government shall pay to the Company the sum of Three hundred thou...
Dominion of Canada.———

Second. The Company to retain all the posts or stations now actually possessed and occupied b...
other part of British North America) and may within twelve months after the acceptance of
posts or stations within any part of British North America not comprised in Canada and
Territory with a List made out by the Company and communicated to the Canadian Mini...
is to be proceeded with with all convenient speed.———

...ll come unto or concern The
...venturers of England trading into Hudson's Bay
... Governor and Company were established and incorporated by their
...dventurers of England trading into Hudson's Bay" by Letters Patent granted
... the Twenty second year of His reign whereby His said Majesty granted unto
...rade and commerce of all those Seas Straits Bays Rivers Lakes Creeks and Sounds
...its together with all the lands and territories upon the Countries Coasts and
...ranted to any of His Majesty's subjects or possessed by the subjects of any
...ne of His Majesty's Plantations or Colonies in America called Ruperts Land
...bsolute Lords and Proprietors of the same Territory Limits and places aforesaid
... and Successors for the same and granted to the said Governor and Company and
...erts Land as therein expressed **And whereas** ever since the date of the
... of such trade and commerce as therein mentioned and have exercised and
... and Company may have exercised or assumed rights of Government in other
...nd **whereas** by the British North America Act 1867 it is (amongst
...dvice of Her Majesty's Most Honorable Privy Council on Address from the
...hem into the Union of the Dominion of Canada on such terms and
...rovisions of the said Act **And whereas** by the Ruperts
..."Ruperts Land" shall include the whole of the lands and Territories
...r the said Governor and Company to surrender to Her Majesty and for
...y of the Lands territories rights privileges liberties franchises and
...nt to the said Governor and Company within Ruperts Land
...d the said Governor and Company provided however that such
... Land shall be admitted into the said Dominion of Canada shall
...es of the Parliament of Canada in pursuance of the 146th Section
... Surrender all rights of Government and proprietary rights
...ported to be granted by the said Letters Patent to the said
...bsolutely extinguished Provided that nothing in the said Act
... Land or elsewhere trade and commerce **And whereas** Her
...onditions upon which the said Governor and Company shall
...Act 1868 contained all the rights of Government and other
...xcept and subject as in the said terms and conditions expressed
...r rights which have been exercised or assumed by the said
... Land or of Canada or of British Columbia in order and to
... the last mentioned Act the said Ruperts Land may be admitted
...ne of them **And whereas** the said terms and conditions
... and Company (who are in the following articles designated as

...d pounds Sterling when Ruperts Land is transferred to the

...m or their Officers or Agents (whether in Ruperts Land or any
...said Surrender select a block of land adjoining each of their
...ritish Columbia in conformity except as regards the Red River
... being the List in the annexed Schedule - The actual Survey

D
DEED OF SURRENDER

Canada's acquisition of Hudson's Bay Company's former territories in 1870 has been likened to the Louisiana Purchase. In exchange for its Charter rights in the west, the Company received £300K in cash as well as extensive land grants which provided its primary source of revenue for the next 50 years. As the region was settled, the Company's business changed inexorably from the fur trade to retail.

L
LAST SPIKE

Considered by many to be the most famous photograph in Canadian history, the driving of the Last Spike occurred November 7, 1885. Canadian Pacific Railway Director Donald Smith did the honours. Smith, who had joined Hudson's Bay Company in 1838, was not only a senior executive with the Company but was also its majority share-holder. His financial backing of the railroad earned him a knighthood in 1886. As Lord Strathcona and Mount Royal, he served as Governor of HBC from 1889 until his death in 1914.

Driving the Golden Spike, by Hon. D. A.

H
HOME DECOR

A Hudson's Bay Company Point Blanket "adds a graphic punch of colour" to this warm and inviting Case Study House (opposite) and to the cover of *Architectural Digest*. Amid the selection of 1950s inspired furniture by George Nelson, Charles Eames, and Isamu Noguchi, an iconic Hudson's Bay Company blanket holds a place of honour in the master bedroom.

A
ARCHITECTURE

Care and craftsmanship are evident in this ornate archway at the Queen Street department store in Toronto. Customer experience is a crucial aspect of the Company's commitment to quality. This extends to the exteriors of its flagship department stores.

J

JASPER AVENUE

William Tomison of Hudson's Bay Company founded Fort Edmonton in the fall of 1795. A key provisioning post, Edmonton steadily grew in importance. The Fort remained in operation for the next 120 years, until completion of the provincial Legislature required its demolition in 1915. Hudson's Bay Company's flagship store at Jasper Ave. and 103rd St., depicted here in 1940, opened in 1913 and operated until 1995 when it relocated to The Edmonton Centre.

H
HOMAGE

Inspiration is the mother of invention. A group of ten Canadian designers were challenged to reinvent the iconic Hudson's Bay Company Point Blanket coat in twenty-first-century style. These contemporary twists on the blanket were created by Harricana (opposite, left), Smythe (opposite, right) and Comrags (this page).

OPPORTUNITY

With the Deed of Surrender in 1870 Hudson's Bay Company acquired vast acreage in western Canada that provided the bulk of its profits for the next fifty years. Related businesses facilitated immigration from Europe and built and sold homes on urban lots.

Awakening Earth   *H. Armstrong Roberts*

FARM LANDS FOR SALE

In Alberta, Saskatchewan, Manitoba

Grain Growing   -   Ranching   -   Mixed Farming

Write for information to

LAND DEPARTMENT, WINNIPEG

Hudson's Bay Company.

INCORPORATED 2ⁿᵈ MAY 1670.

E

EDGY

Captivating consumers of all ages and styles, The Bay stores offer a smartly curated mix of accessories for the young and fashionable, such as this clutch purse by Brian Atwood.

H

HAT

By the late seventeenth century, beavers—the main source of felt for gentlemen's hats—had been hunted to near extinction in Europe. Enter the Canadian beaver, with its thick, lustrous fur. Suddenly, milliners everywhere were demanding Hudson's Bay Company furs from the New World.

G

GLOVES

Cutting a dapper figure in his capote and fur gauntlets, Prince Arthur, first Duke of Connaught and Strathearn, is proudly dressed for the elements. For centuries, Hudson's Bay Company outerwear, such as coats, hats, and gloves, has kept Canadians warm and dry.

M
MODERNISM

In the postwar boom of the 1950s, Canadians gathered in communities called suburbs. Where the shoppers went, Hudson's Bay Company followed, opening gleaming new suburban stores such as this Mississauga, Ontario, location. These new sites had a distinctly modern design aesthetic.

T

THE ROOM

Where Canada and couture connect, The Room—
The Bay's high-end Toronto fashion salon—features
ready-to-wear and runway pieces from some of the
world's most coveted designers. First opened in 1937
as the St. Regis Room at Simpsons, it was relaunched
in 2009 to universal acclaim.

C

CANADA 2010

With its 2010 Olympic Team Retail Apparel collection, Hudson's Bay Company redefined the concept of Canadian cool. And when the world's eyes turned to Vancouver for the Winter Games, Hudson's Bay Company was the clear gold medal winner for style.

B

BLANKET

Traded on traplines, sought after in cities, the Hudson's Bay Company Point Blanket has, for more than two centuries, epitomized elegance, endurance and warmth. Introduced in 1780 and woven from the finest British and New Zealand wools, these iconic blankets—still available for purchase today—are heirlooms to be passed down through generations.

H
HOCKEY

This squad of eager "Beavers" seems ready to skate to victory. The Hudson's Bay Beavers hockey team of Saskatchewan was just one of a host of Company-sponsored sports teams.

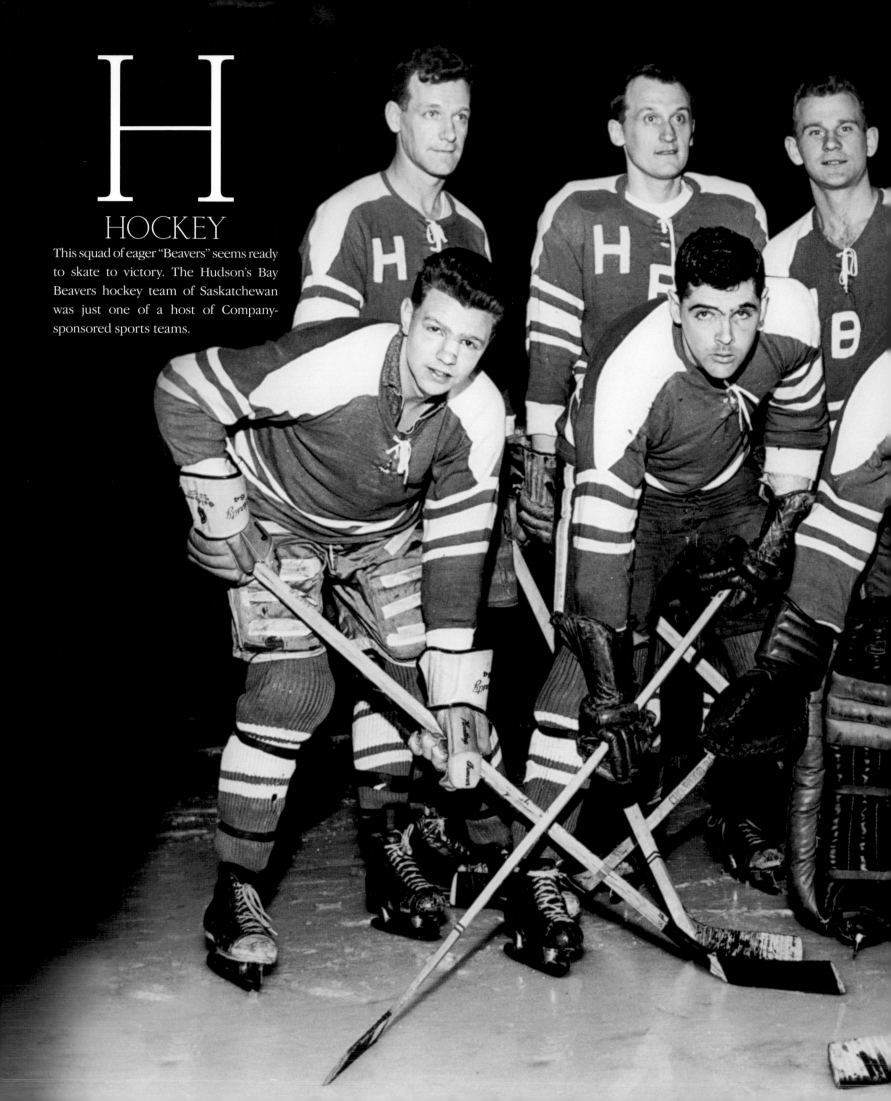

A
ATHLETE

As the official outfitter of the Canadian Olympic Team, Hudson's Bay Company is a key supporter of Canada's amateur athletes. It proudly donated millions of dollars to fund training during the run-up to the Vancouver 2010 Winter Games. Canadian athletes responded by winning more gold medals than any other host nation in the history of the Winter Olympics.

OLYMPICS

What says "Canada" more than toques, scarves, and red mittens? When Hudson's Bay Company unveiled its Canadian Olympic Team Apparel at the 2010 Vancouver Winter Games, it owned the podium in terms of fashion. Hudson's Bay Company also dressed Canadian athletes at the 2006 Torino Winter Games and the 2008 Summer Games, in Beijing.

V
VANCOUVER

Opened in 1914, The Bay at Granville and Georgia streets in downtown Vancouver transformed the retail experience for shoppers. One of six original Hudson's Bay Company department stores modelled on Harrods of London, the store symbolized Hudson's Bay Company's commitment to expanding its retail operations.

M
MODERN CLASSIC

As cities grow and change retail changes along with them. Sometimes that means the retail district itself relocates, as happened in Saskatoon, Saskatchewan. Today the former Hudson's Bay Company store, which underwent a major renovation in 1968, is a heritage building, home to high-end condominums.

PARADE

Resplendent in their Hudson's Bay Point Blanket coats, the Canadian Winter Olympic team marches into the outdoor stadium in Innsbruck, Austria, during the Opening Ceremonies of the 1964 Winter Olympic Games. The provision of outerwear to the winter Olympic teams of the 1960s helped popularize the Company's iconic stripes as a symbol of Canada around the world.

N
NORTHERN LIGHTS

Dressed in white tunics bearing the iconic colours of the Hudson's Bay Company Point Blanket, three elk-men welcome the arrival of the majestic aurora borealis in Janet Stahle-Fraser's *Three Auroras*. According to the Algonquin people, Nanahbozho, the Creator, after he finished creating the earth, travelled to the far north. There he builds great fires which reflect southward, reminding those he created of his lasting love.

F

FEMININITY

From frills to florals, the dress collection at The Bay is renowned for its charm and fantasy. One of a cohort of new Canadian designers taking the fashion world by storm, the Montreal-born Erdem Moralioglu is famed for his radical reinventions of floral prints (this page), while the visionary designer Christophe Decarnin is breaking new ground at Balmain (opposite), the French fashion house that made its name as the postwar outfitter of stars such as Ava Gardner and Brigitte Bardot.

W

WINNIPEG

Situated at the heart of the continent, Winnipeg, Manitoba, has played a central role in the development of Hudson's Bay Company. The site of major forts, including Upper Fort Garry, it was the company's Canadian headquarters for six decades. Today the city is home to the Hudson's Bay Company Archives and the Hudson's Bay Company Museum Collection at The Manitoba Museum.

C

CANOE

Invented by First Nations peoples and adopted by European explorers, the canoe is symbolic of both Canada and Hudson's Bay Company. Travelling thousands of kilometres along rivers and lakes, the early fur traders rewrote the maps of North America with every stroke of their paddles.

THE OLYMPIC STORE 🍁 LA BOUTIQUE OLYMPIQUE

S
SPIRIT

The soaring colours of sea and sky dress the 2010 Winter Games Olympic Superstore at The Bay, downtown Vancouver. Retail headquarters for official Games-related merchandise, the store occupied the entire main floor of the 96-year-old flagship and won no less than four major design awards.

P

POST

With the stark mountains of Frobisher Bay, Northwest Territories, looming in the background, a Hudson's Bay Company trading post employee shares a moment in 1956 with an Inuit boy. After a century on Hudson and James Bays, Hudson's Bay Company established its first inland outpost in 1774 at Cumberland House in Saskatchewan. With the establishment of each subsequent trading post, another region of Canada was opened up to the trade.

GEORGIAN ROOM
Afternoon Tea
Menu

THE NONSUCH

Hudson's Bay Company.
INCORPORATED 2ND MAY 1670.

No. 2

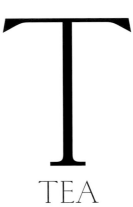

T
TEA

The Company's first shipment of tea, from London to York Factory, took place in 1716. Initially provided for its staff, the First Nations soon acquired a taste for the world's favourite pick-me-up. By the early 20th century Hudson's Bay Company was packing its own branded teas and coffees for sale in its stores, and serving it to tired customers in its restaurants.

B
BEST PROCURABLE

Hudson's Bay Company private branded liquor was a significant ancillary business for most of the 20th century. A full range of spirits was available to discerning Canadian hosts.

E
EDMONTON

The Alberta capital is just one of several major communities that owes its start to Hudson's Bay. An employee, William Tomison, founded Fort Edmonton in the fall of 1795. The Company's first retail store there opened in 1890 and was followed by one of the original six flagship department stores in 1913.

F
FIRST IMPRESSIONS

Historically the main floor—like that of the Vancouver store, shown here—is where the retailer must capture the customer's attention. Lavish displays of aspirational items such as fragrance, beauty, jewellery, and accessories entice customers and invite them to explore further.

S
STRIPES

While the iconic multistripe pattern is the most famous, Hudson's Bay Company Point Blankets have been produced in many hues over the years. What we today consider the "traditional" order of the stripes—green, red, yellow, and indigo—didn't become standardized until the mid-to-late nineteenth century.

Y

YORK FACTORY

Gateway to Rupert's Land, York Factory on the shores of Hudson Bay in northern Manitoba was the hub of Hudson's Bay Company's operations for more than two hundred years. Built in 1884, today, thanks to its donation by Hudson's Bay Company, York Factory is a Canadian National Historic Site.

HUDSON'S BAY COMPANY HISTORY TIMELINE

FOUNDING THE COMPANY

1666   **Radisson** and **des Groseilliers** travel to London, where they receive sponsorship of Prince Rupert and meet his cousin King Charles II.

1668   A speculative voyage leaves London. A storm damages the *Eaglet*, which is forced to turn back, but the ***Nonsuch*** reaches Hudson Bay intact.

1668   A first fort, **Charles Fort** (later **Rupert House**; now **Waskaganish**), is built at the mouth of Rupert River, James Bay.

1669   *Nonsuch* returns to England with the first cargo of fur resulting from trade in Hudson Bay—worth £1,380.

1670   On May 2, **King Charles II** grants the initial group of investors—the "Governor and Company of Adventurers of England Trading into Hudson Bay"—a **Royal Charter** allowing them a monopoly to trade in the Hudson Bay drainage basin.

1672   The Company's first public sale of furs—27 lots—is held at **Garraway's Coffee House.**

1673   **Moose Factory** is established.

1679   **Albany Fort** is established.

1680   **Severn House** is established.

1684   **York Factory** is established.

FROM THE SHORES OF HUDSON BAY

1690   **Henry Kelsey** embarks on a two-year journey of exploration that will make him the first white man to see the buffalo herds of the prairies.

1713   **Treaty of Utrecht**. France relinquishes all claims to Hudson Bay, which again becomes a British possession.

1745 British Parliament offers £20,000 for discovery of the **Northwest Passage** and £5,000 for reaching the North Pole.

1754 **Anthony Henday** travels inland from York Factory to "draw down many of the natives to trade." He journeys via the Saskatchewan River as far as the Rocky Mountain foothills and is the first to meet the Blackfoot tribes.

1771 **Samuel Hearne** travels to the Arctic Ocean in search of copper.

1774 Samuel Hearne completes building of Hudson's Bay Company's first inland post, **Cumberland House**, near Pine Island Lake of the Saskatchewan River.

RIVALRY AND COMPETITION

1779 **North West Company** founded in Montreal as a seasonal partnership. The company becomes a permanent entity in 1783.

1780 Thomas Empson, a weaver based in Witney, Oxfordshire, England, is contracted to make the first **Point Blankets**.

1795 **Fort Edmonton** is founded.

1803 **North West Company** opens its fur depot in Lachine, near Montreal.

1811 **Thomas Douglas**, **Lord Selkirk**, majority shareholder of Hudson's Bay Company, purchases more than seventy-four million acres in the Red River Valley from the Company for the sum of ten shillings. He plans to use the land to settle displaced Scottish Highlanders. The first settlers arrive the following year.

1821 **Hudson's Bay Company** merges with its main rival, the **North West Company**, based in Montreal, and is granted a twenty-one-year monopoly under the Hudson's Bay Company name; Hudson's Bay Company controls three million square miles of land (7.77 million sq. km) and operates 173 posts.

1821 **George Simpson** becomes governor of the Northern Department.

FROM SEA TO SEA TO SEA

1825   **Fort Vancouver** is founded on the Columbia River to serve as the Pacific headquarters of the Company.

1827   **Fort Langley** is established, the first Hudson's Bay Company post on the coast of British Columbia.

1831   **Lower Fort Garry** is established.

1836   ***S.S. Beaver*** is the first steamship in the Pacific Northwest. It is in service with Hudson's Bay Company until 1863, when it is leased to the government for surveying. It is wrecked off Stanley Park in 1888.

1838   **Donald Alexander Smith** joins Hudson's Bay Company as a clerk grading muskrat pelts at Lachine.

1840   **Puget Sound Agricultural Company** formed as a joint stock company to develop agricultural businesses and settlement in the Oregon Country. PSAC's stockholders are Hudson's Bay Company directors and senior officers.

1843   **Fort Victoria** is built.

1849   Hudson's Bay Company's Pacific headquarters moved from **Fort Vancouver** to Fort Victoria, since the former is now in U.S. territory.

1854   Hudson's Bay Company man **Dr. John Rae** maps the final sections of the Arctic coastline, discovering both the missing link of the Northwest Passage and the fate of the Franklin Expedition.

1860   Death of **Sir George Simpson**.

1870   Hudson's Bay Company returns sovereignty of Rupert's Land back to the Crown via a **Deed of Surrender**. The Crown then transfers it to Canada. Hudson's Bay Company receives a cash settlement of £300,000 and considerable land concessions.

THE RISE OF RETAIL

1880   Hudson's Bay Company begins to sell farm lots in western Canada.

1880   Main Hudson's Bay Company Canadian office moved from Montreal to Winnipeg; land boom begins in Winnipeg.

1881   First Hudson's Bay Company mail order catalogue produced.

1887   Earliest known date for Hudson's Bay Company's operation of steamship transportation of goods and people on the major waterways of western Canada.

1889   Hudson's Bay Company, CPR, and federal government push land sales in the west.

1889   **Sir Donald Alexander Smith** becomes twenty-sixth governor of Hudson's Bay Company.

1907   Hudson's Bay Company establishes the **Wholesale Department** to sell liquor, tobacco, coffee, tea, confectionery, and blankets.

1909   Fur Trade Commissioner Ralph Parsons establishes Hudson's Bay Company's first post in the eastern Arctic at Cape Wolstenholme.

1909   **Richard Burbidge** of Harrods joins Hudson's Bay Company Director Leonard Cunliffe on an inspection tour of Hudson's Bay Company retail stores in Canada. His report recommends the division of the Company's operations into three separate departments: Fur Trade, Land Sales, Retailing.

1911   Hudson's Bay Company commissions the building of the ***S.S. Nascopie***, forms The Nascopie Steamship Company Ltd. with Job Brothers of St. John's to own and operate it.

1912   Hudson's Bay Company Board names the Canadian Advisory Committee to advise on overseas growth. First members Sir Augustus Nanton, George Galt, and Sir William Whyte are eminent businessmen based in Winnipeg.

Lights of a City Street by Frederick M. Bell Smith

| 1913 | Hudson's Bay Company opens new modern department stores in Calgary and Edmonton, the first of six flagship stores planned in response to the Burbidge inspection tour. |

1914   **Hudson's Bay Company Governor Donald Alexander Smith**, **Lord Strathcona and Mount Royal**, dies at the age of ninety-three.

1915-1919   Hudson's Bay Company participates in war effort, chartering three hundred vessels to transport foodstuffs, fuel, lumber, and munitions as agent for the French government.

DIVERSIFICATION

1920   **250th anniversary**. Celebrations include a visit to Canada by Governor **Sir Robert Molesworth Kindersley**, production of a book, a limited-edition commemorative medal, and the establishment of *The Beaver* as an in-house magazine.

1920   First establishment of Newfoundland fishery. Hudson's Bay Company begins to produce "Hubay" and "Labdor" canned salmon following its proprietary method that constitutes a major improvement over pickled salmon.

1920   Hudson's Bay Company acquires Cairns and expands in Saskatchewan and operates as Hudson's Bay Company.

1921   Hudson's Bay Company enters into an agreement with **Imperial Oil Company** to exploit Hudson's Bay Company mineral rights on all lands sold since 1910 in Manitoba, Alberta, and Saskatchewan.

1923   As part of a strategy to develop fur collection outside Canada, the Company obtains under license the monopoly to buy furs collected in Siberia.

1925   Beaver House, Garlick Hill, opens in London. Constructed as world's largest fur auction house.

1926   Partners with Marland Oil Company of America to form **Hudson's Bay Marland Oil Company**.

1926   Hudson's Bay Company Overseas Settlement (Limited) formed to facilitate immigration.

1929	**Hudson's Bay Oil and Gas Company** formed.
1930	Beaver in northern Quebec are disappearing and the Cree are starving as a result. **Maud Watt**, wife of Rupert House post factor **Jimmy Watt**, travels by foot, dogsled, and train to Quebec City where she convinces the provincial government of the need for a beaver preserve. She returns with a lease to more than 18,000 square kilometres.
1930	**Canadian Committee's** powers extended to oversee all day-to-day operations of the Company in Canada.
1932	Hudson's Bay Company introduces airplanes to deliver goods to Northern Canada, reducing ocean vessels to one steamer and several coastal and river vessels.
1934	Hudson's Bay Company hires Professor Coupland of Oxford University and Hilary Jenkinson of the British Public Record Office to review the archival collection and prepare catalogues.
1936	A record **thirty thousand** Arctic fox pelts are exported by Hudson's Bay Company from the north.
1943	Hudson's Bay Company-managed beaver sanctuaries in Quebec, Ontario, and the Northwest Territories cover more than 100 thousand square kilometres.
1944	First Hudson's Bay Company Scholarships awarded (two in England and two in Canada) to commemorate the 275th anniversary and encourage education in administrative and commercial subjects.
1945	Transfers all real estate holdings except Fur Posts and Land Department to wholly owned subsidiary **Rupert's Land Trading Co**.
1951	Hudson's Bay Company becomes the supplier of Inuit art to the Canadian Handicrafts Guild.
1953	Hudson's Bay Company winds up its Land Department.
1955	First parking garage of any Hudson's Bay Company store built in Edmonton.
1959	Fur Trade Division renamed Northern Stores Department.

RETAIL ACQUISITION

1960   Hudson's Bay Company arrives in eastern Canada through acquisition of Montreal-based **Henry Morgan & Co. Ltd.**'s ten-store chain; converts its Ontario stores to the Hudson's Bay name, but keeps the Quebec stores operating under the Morgan's name until 1972.

1965   Hudson's Bay Company introduces "**The Bay**" banner, converting its retail stores to the new brand.

1969   **York Factory** donated to Canada as a National Historic Site.

1970   **Three hundredth anniversary** celebrations. *Nonsuch* replica is shipped from England to Canada where it tours the east and west coasts in 1971. Afterward the replica becomes the first significant donation by the Company to the Manitoba Museum.

1970   Hudson's Bay Company becomes a Canadian company and Head Office is moved from London to Winnipeg.

1972   Hudson's Bay Company acquires Ottawa retailer **A.J. Freiman**, Limited, and converts its stores to The Bay banner.

1972   Acquisition of Shop-Rite, a four-store catalogue chain.

1973   Acquisition of 64.1 percent of Markborough Properties.

1974   Opening of the 260,000-square-foot store and thirty-five-storey office tower at Yonge and Bloor. Head Office relocates to Toronto.

1977   The Company starts installing computerized cash registers in stores.

1978   The **Staff House at Moose Factory** is turned over to the Province of Ontario. Today the Staff House is part of the Centennial Park Museum.

1978   Acquisition of prestige store group **Simpsons** and **35.6 percent interest in Simpsons-Sears**. Hudson's Bay Company maintains Simpsons as a subsidiary and later folds stores into The Bay.

1978	Acquisition of **Zellers** and Fields, a Zellers Company. Hudson's Bay Company maintains Zellers as a wholly owned subsidiary; Zellers maintains Fields as a wholly owned subsidiary.
1979	Kenneth Thomson acquires 75 percent of Hudson's Bay Company common shares.
1981	Sale of **Hudson's Bay Oil and Gas** to **Dome Resources**.
1982	Hudson's Bay Company closes its Shop-Rite Catalogue store chain.
1982	First word processor at The Bay head office, Toronto.
1983	Hudson's Bay Company disposes of its 35.6 percent interest in Simpsons-Sears.
1984	Hudson's Bay & Annings, Hudson's Bay Company Fur Sales Canada Ltd., and Hudson's Bay Company Fur Sales Incorporated, selling furs in London, Montreal, and New York, are reorganized into a single entity operating in all three locales under the name **Hudson's Bay Company Fur Sales International Ltd.**
1987	Hudson's Bay Company sells its **Wholesale Division**.
1987	**Northern Stores Division** is sold to a group of investors, including 415 employees. Hudson's Bay Company ceases to deal in the acquisition of pelts. Three years later, the new company revives the North West Company name.
1993	Hudson's Bay Company acquires **Woodward's** and converts most of its stores to Bay or Zellers stores.
1994	Donation of Hudson's Bay Company records to the **Hudson's Bay Company Archives**.
1994	Publication of *The Beaver* magazine is taken over by Canada's National History Society (CNHS).
1998	Zellers acquires Kmart Canada and converts its stores to Zellers stores.

1999	Hudson's Bay Company launches new **Home Outfitters** store chain.
2000	Hudson's Bay Company launches **hbc.com**.
2001	Hudson's Bay Company launches **HBC Rewards**.
2003	Hudson's Bay Company launches new Hudson's Bay Company Signature brand, a line of apparel and accessories directly inspired by the Company's rich history.
2005	Hudson's Bay Company chosen **Premier National Partner for the Olympic Games** through 2012.
2007	The Hudson's Bay Company Archives collection is added to UNESCO's **Memory of the World Register**.
2008	Incorporation of the Hudson's Bay Company in 1670 named the number one business event in Canadian history.
2010	Hudson's Bay Company launches its official Twitter account: thehudsonsbayco.

Opposite: What better way to spend a sunny summer day in 1965 than to swing over to the Morgan's department store in Ottawa?

LEADERSHIP TIMELINE

1670-1682	His Highness Prince Rupert of the Rhine
1683-1685	HRH Prince James, Duke of York (later King James II)
1685-1692	John, Lord Churchill (later 1st Duke of Marlborough)
1692-1696	Sir Stephen Evans
1696-1700	Rt. Hon. Sir William Trumbull
1700-1712	Sir Stephen Evans
1712-1743	Sir Bibye Lake, Bart.
1743-1746	Benjamin Pitt
1746-1750	Thomas Knapp
1750-1760	Sir Atwell Lake, Bart.
1760-1770	Sir William Baker
1770-1782	Bibye Lake
1782-1799	Samuel Wegg
1799-1807	Sir James Winter Lake, Bart.
1807-1812	William Mainwaring
1812-1822	Joseph Berens, Jr.
1822-1852	Sir John Henry Pelly, Bart.
1852-1856	Andrew Colvile
1856-1858	John Shepherd
1858-1863	Henry Hulse Berens

1863-1868	Rt. Hon. Sir Edmund Walker Head, Bart., K.C.B.
1868-1869	Rt. Hon. John, Lord Wodehouse, 1st Earl of Kimberley
1869-1874	Rt. Hon. Sir Stafford Northcote, Bart., M.P., later 1st Earl of Iddesleigh
1874-1880	Rt. Hon. George Joachim Goschen, M.P.
1880-1889	Eden Colvile
1889-1914	Donald A. Smith, Baron Strathcona and Mount Royal, G.C.M.G.
1914-1915	Sir Thomas Skinner, Bart.
1915-1925	Sir Robert Molesworth Kindersley
1925-1931	Charles Vincent Sale
1931-1952	Sir Patrick Ashley Cooper
1952-1965	William Johnston Keswick
1965-1970	Rt. Hon. Derick Heathcoat Amory, Viscount Amory
1970-1982	George T. Richardson
1982-1994	Donald Scott McGiverin
1994-1997	David E. Mitchell, O.C.
1997-2006	Yves L. Fortier, C.C., Q.C.
2006-2008	Jerry Zucker
2008	Anita Zucker
2008-PRESENT	Richard A. Baker

INDEX

CREDITS

All images © Hudson's Bay Company Archives, Archives of Manitoba, except the following:

Page 6: Walter J. Phillips/Hudson's Bay Company; page 23: © Franz Rosenbaum/courtesy of Stephen Bulger Gallery; page 25: © Bolton Museum and Art Gallery, Lancashire, UK/Bridgeman Art Library; page 28: Adam Sheriff Scott/Hudson's Bay Company; page 29: © Shot by Fuel Advertising; page 32-33: City of Toronto Archives, Fonds 1244, Item 7.10; page 38-39: © George Pimentel; page 40-41: © 20th Century Fox, ™ and ©/courtesy of Everett Collection; page 42-43: City of Toronto Archives, Fonds 1244, Item 38.21; page 47: Walter J. Phillips/Hudson's Bay Company; page 48-49: © Archives of Ontario; page 54: Adam Sheriff Scott/Hudson's Bay Company; page 58: Jeremey Powell, Canadian Conservation Institute, Department of Canadian Heritage © Government of Canada; page 59: © Institute for Information Technology, National Research Council; page 65: © Laziz Hamani; page 66-67, 68-69: © George Pimentel; page 72-73: © Raymond Meier/trunkarchive.com; page 74-75: © Laziz Hamani; page 78: © Doug Levitt/Hudson's Bay Company; page 79: Adam Sherriff Scott/Hudson's Bay Company; page 80: © Fox Photos/Getty Images; page 84-85: Ronald Searle/Hudson's Bay Company; page 86-87: Courtesy of A.W. Hainsworth & Sons Ltd.; page 90: courtesy of Nicoli Garner and Jessica Weirmier; page 91: Courtesy of Harold Tichenor; page 94-95: Will Davies/Hudson's Bay Company; page 97: © Library and Archives Canada, Acc. No. 1957-101; page 102: © Bridgeman Art Library; page 106-107: Charles Comfort/Hudson's Bay Company; page 108-109: © Library and Archives Canada/C-033945; page 111: © Frank Veronsky; page 118: © George Pimentel; page 119: © Evan Dion Photography; page 122-123: © George Pimentel; Page 132-133: © Getty Images; page 144: Illustration by Ronald Searle/Hudson's Bay Company; page 145: © Library and Archives Canada, Acc. No. 1984-209-1; page 148: Adolphus Muller-Ury/Hudson's Bay Company; page 149: © Sir Geoffrey Kneller/Hudson's Bay Company; page 152: © Don Knight; page 154-155: © Transcendental Graphics/Getty Images; page 159: © Digital Vision/Getty Images; page 160-161: © Michael Cooper/Raj Prem Collection; page 166: scanned from original owned by Paul Minard; page 181: © Ross Durant Photography/Getty Images; page 188-189, 192: © McCord Museum; page 194: © Kevin O'Brien/courtesy of *Fashion* magazine; page 198-199: © Shot by Fuel Advertising; 200-201: © The National Archives of the UK, ref.CO42/694; page 202-203: Library and Archives Canada/Alexander Ross/C-003693; page 204: Dominique Vorillon/www.dominiquevorillon.com, Waltzer Residence/www.kathrynwaltzer.com, originally published in Canadian *House & Home* Magazine; page 205: *Architectural Digest*/Condé Nast Archive © Condé Nast; page 210-211: © Geoffrey Barrenger; page 213: courtesy of Brian Atwood/BPCM; page 214: © Library and Archives Canada/Detail of C-017338; page 215: © McCord Museum; page 218-219: © George Pimentel; page 220-221: © Gabor Jurina/www.kathiz.com; page 227: © Clay Enos; page 228-229: © Getty Images; page 234-235: © Don Knight; page 236-237: © Janet Stahle-Fraser; page 238: © John Huba/Art + Commerce; page 239: © Regan Cameron/Art + Commerce; page 242-243: courtesy of the Canadian Canoe Museum; page 245-246: © Ed White Photographer; page 246-247: © Library and Archives Canada/Gavin White, Fonds/PA-166341; page 248: © Jens Mortensen/Hudson's Bay Company; page 258-259: © Kevin Fleming; page 264-265: Frederick M. Bell-Smith/Hudson's Bay Company.

ACKNOWLEDGMENTS

Many people made this work possible: Patrick Dickinson, Jessica Johnson, and Michele Cortese of The Bay Marketing; Debbie Keffer of HBC Heritage Services; the Hudson's Bay Company Archives in Winnipeg; and the team at Assouline including Esther Kremer, Nicole Lanctot, Camille Dubois, Cécilia Maurin, Céline Bouchez, Rebecca Stepler, and Naomi Leibowitz. Don Knight, Nicoli Garner, and Jessica Weirmier graciously gave permission to use their personal photographs. A special thanks for the cooperation and support of The Bay's Executive Leadership under the direction of President and CEO Bonnie Brooks.

CANADA, ou

NOU-

DU

Port Bourbon

LAC DES POUX

LAC DES ASSINIBOUELS

LAC DES CHRISTINAUX

Rivière Bourbon

Rivière S.ᵗᵉ Therese

NOM

FR-

NATIONS SOUS LE

Fort la Tourette

Lac Alepimigon

D'OUTA-

NATION DES SIOUX

Lac de Buade

C

OU-

LAC

SUPERIEUR

LAC N

LAC

SAINT ANTOINE

Fort S. Antoine

Fort S. Croix

ACS

LAC

DES

ILINOIS

DES

HURONS

Fort Duluo S.ᵗ Joseph

L'AC ERIE

MASCOUTENS

NATION

DU

FEU

Fort Chicagou

LES

PANI-

PANIETOUCA

RIVIERE

DES ILINOIS

Fort S. Louis

Fort Crevecœur

Lac Pontcho

CON-

TREE

RIVIERE

MAHA

MISSOURI

DES ILINOIS

OHIO, ou

BELLE RIVIERE

OHIO ou BELLE RIVIERE

LES KASKINAME

GATAKA

OUPAPA

La Grande Rivière des Missou

PANIMAHA

PANA l'Épée

PANEASSA

CANSA ou Emissourites

DE

LA

LOUI-

LES PANE-

ASSA les Voleurs

OHIO, ou BELLE RIVIERE

Fort bâti pour la prise des Cicacha

CAROLINE, ou

FLORIDE DE FRANÇOIS

PAYS ET IS-LES

CHEPOUSSEA

MISSISIPI

S

FLEUVE

MISSISIPI

CICACHA 3 Villages

SI A-

DES A CANCEA

N-

FLORIDE

ICOUKKEA

LAZOU

TOUNICA

TAENSA

NATCHE

KOROA

OUMNA

CAP

DE LA

FLORIDE

DE MEX.